How to \
and Se n
Great Short
Stories

How to Write and Sell Great Short Stories

Linda M. James

COMPASS BOOKS

Winchester, UK
Washington, USA

First published by Compass Books, 2011
Compass Books is an imprint of John Hunt Publishing Ltd., Laurel House, Station Approach,
Alresford, Hants, SO24 9JH, UK
office1@o-books.net
www.o-books.com

For distributor details and how to order please visit the 'Ordering' section on our website.

Text copyright: Linda M. James 2010

ISBN: 978 1 84694 716 2

A CIP catalogue record for this book is available from the British Library.

Design: Stuart Davies

Printed in the UK by CPI Antony Rowe
Printed in the USA by Offset Paperback Mfrs, Inc

We operate a distinctive and ethical publishing philosophy in all
areas of our business, from our global network of authors to
production and worldwide distribution.

CONTENTS

This book is dedicated to writers everywhere.

'Now that we have seen each other,' said the Unicorn, 'if you'll believe in me, I'll believe in you...'
From "Through The Looking Glass" by Lewis Carroll

'Imagination is more important than knowledge.'
Albert Einstein.

Acknowledgements

The author would like to thank David Higham Associates for their kind permission to reproduce a short extract from Alice Walker's book "The Color Purple" which was published by Orion Books in 1982.

The author would also like to thank the writer Susan Gibb for allowing her short story "Wanderer" to be reproduced in this book. Susan won first prize for this story in the 2010 'Glass Woman's Prize' competition.

Introduction

What's the difference between a man thinking about death and a man making his own coffin? One sounds like a philosophical tract; the other has all the essence of a fascinating story. Why? Because the man building his own coffin intrigues us. What sort of man makes his own coffin? Why is he making it now? Is he about to die soon or is he preparing for the future? It opens up possibilities which the writer must explore to produce a memorable story.

But how do you know you've written one? Read it aloud and stop half way through. If your audience say 'You can't stop - what happens next?' You've succeeded; you've teased your reader with small hooking details and your audience is desperate to know more. And that's the secret of story-telling in a nutshell – curiosity. We love to know what will happen next. That's why children's eyes widen when Little Red Riding Hood walks in the woods; they are afraid for her and want her to be safe. All the writer has to do is to make the reader wait to find out if she is. The essence of writing a memorable story is to place three-dimensional characters within a vivid location and give them a number of complications they must try to resolve. Easy, isn't it? Well, it can be, if you know how to do it.

The following pages will show you how to write stories that will have your reader eager to turn over the page to find out what happens next.

Chapter 1

Creating Memorable Characters

As a small child I thought my Welsh grandmother must have invented people because she knew so much about them. While other people read books: my grandmother read tea-leaves; from these strange marooned squiggles lying at the bottom of tea cups, she seemed to discover more about people's lives than Charles Dickens ever did from wandering endlessly around the streets of London. When I was ten, I plucked up the courage to ask her how she did it - she told me she was clairvoyant. I was puzzled, wondering why she called herself Clare Voyant when her real name was Sarah Jones. And what did her answer have to do with my question, anyway? I never managed to pluck up the courage to ask her again and even if I had, I wouldn't have had the opportunity as the adults in my family talked all the time. Welsh children from large families were taught that silence was golden. [Or at least a faded shade of ochre.] At ten, I thought the adults must be making up for hours of enforced childhood silence by talking endlessly. A gathering of sometimes ten or fifteen animated, loud Welsh voices in a small room forced me into a world of fantasy where I could wander unnoticed for hours. There I created people who I would use years later as an adult.

All of us have people from the past and present walking around in our heads waiting to written about. Here are some ways to make them *seem* real.

Caring About Characters.
Have you ever read a story and given up half way through because you're really not interested? The characters seem one-dimensional and do things that you don't believe they'd do.

We've all read stories like that and the reason we become bored is because the writer doesn't really know his/her characters well enough to make them convincing. Knowing your characters intimately is vital when writing engaging stories. If we're not interested in them, why should we care if they fall off a cliff/ their partner leaves them or their cat dies? Your readers must care about the characters you create otherwise why should they waste their valuable time on them? I remember asking one of my students many years ago to tell me about one of the characters in his story. He told me his character was 45, married and lived in Hastings. A good start, I thought. He knows three things about him. Then, after I'd read his story, I discovered that these three things were the only things he did know. Because he didn't know his character well, his character's actions weren't authentic and therefore his plot wasn't credible. You must know your characters better than you know your best friend; better than you know yourself, in fact.

Shallow characterisation is one of the reasons why so many stories are rejected which is why I wrote the following question-naire. The following questions are going to be very useful to you when you create people; real people with desires, fears and flaws. It's an exciting process. Imagine, you're going to create another human being without a partner!

Please read through the following questions and answer them to create a convincing human being. [For clarity I have used a male character.]

Character Biography
1.   What is his age and name?
2.   What is his height, build, colour of hair, eyes and skin?
3.   Does he have any facial expressions, a squint or any disability? Does he wear glasses or contact lenses?

4. How does he walk or move? Does he have any mannerisms or habits? Does he smoke? If he doesn't, what is his attitude towards people who do?

5. What type of clothes is he comfortable in? Does he change his clothes often?

6. How does he speak? What's the pitch and speed of his voice? Any favourite sayings or words? Does he use slang or swear?

7. Does he live alone or with other people? Does he have any children? What is his relationship to them? What are his children like, if he has any?

8. Where does he live? Does he own his home? How is it furnished? Is he domesticated, tidy or messy?

9. Is he successful in material terms? Does he have a good job with enough money or is he worried about his finances? Is he financially independent?

10. Does he like his job? If not, what would he rather do?

11. Are his parents living? Does he like them? What has he inherited from them both physically and psychologically?

12. What kind of education did he have? Did his parents expect too much or too little from him?

13. What is his nationality? Does he live in his country of origin? If not, why not? How does he feel about this?

14. When he is at home for an evening alone, is he happy with his own company? What does he do? What sort of music does he like, if any?

15. What sort of personality does he have? How does he express tension? How does he express pleasure? How does he express anger?

16. Do people like him? Do people respect him?

17. What does he like most about himself? What does he like least? Does he want to change himself in any way?

18. What does he want out of life? What is he prepared to do to get it?

Why do I need to answer so many questions about a character before I write a story, I hear you ask? Because then you will know exactly how he thinks, speaks and acts in every situation. This is vitally important. Once you really know your character he will start thinking, speaking and acting for himself, not being manipulated by you. In fact, this technique is so effective that sometimes a character will actually speak to you. Uh-oh, I hear you thinking, this woman has definitely lost her marbles. [Now where did that strange expression come from?] She hears voices in her head and now she's telling us to do the same! I know it sounds bizarre, but 'hearing a character's voice' actually happens if you've breathed life into him.

This happened to me one night when I was writing a scene from my WWII novel called "The Invisible Piper". It was a cold, windy night, rather like the weather in my novel. (Interestingly, I've only just realised that the weather outside my window was being mirrored in my writing.) Charlie, my disarming, cheeky ten-year-old evacuee was listening outside a door to his foster-parents' lounge because they were discussing him. (How many of us listen to things we shouldn't?) They were discussing the fact that he would have to be evacuated again as the government thought that evacuees from London weren't safe there. (Germans were 'tipping' their unused bombs over Hastings before returning to Germany.) However, Charlie had discovered that the local children weren't going to be evacuated and he entered the room [against my wishes!] to say he wouldn't go. This kid took over my plot because he decided that he wasn't going to move again from people he had come to love. He told me this quite clearly when I was writing him out of the scene. I heard his voice whisper in my ear saying 'I won't go, so it's useless trying to make me.' That's how alive a character can become if you dig deep enough into his personality!

Naturally, you won't need to use the answers to every question I've asked in every story, but you should learn as much as you can about your characters because once you know exactly how they think, move and act, they become living, breathing human beings. Then when you've learned everything about them, you can often use a 'snap-shot' to introduce them. E.g. 'Imogene was the sort of woman who used men like other women use toilet cleaners.' Readers discover from this pithy sentence exactly how abrasive Imogene is with men and will be able to create their own picture of her.

Once you discover exactly what makes a character tick, you will be able to create interesting, but flawed people. Flaws are important because every character needs both internal and external conflicts to be three-dimensional. Flaws are what make people fascinating and credible. Work through the questionnaire to discover what your character's flaws are. But remember that we all have ways of disguising our flaws, don't we? E.g. Say your character has an Obsessive Compulsive Disorder. That's her internal conflict; each time she leaves the house she has to go back to check that she's locked the door numerous times. However, she can't show people at work because she might lose her job, so can you think of a way she could disguise this flaw? That's her external conflict. Once you've worked out what your characters' internal and external conflicts are they will become three-dimensional.

Okay, I'm going to assume that you've created your first flawed character so now I'd like you to create another dissimilar person. For example, you could create an old bee-keeper and a child from a privileged family, as Susan Hill did in her insightful story "The Boy Who Taught The Bee-keeper to Read". I'm sure you can think of many dissimilar, interesting characters yourself.

Characters and Relationships.

Susan Hill's story shows you how characters interact with each other. I.e. their relationships. But of course, there are many different types of relationships. Try to discover the 'chemistry' between these people. How one main character relates, for example, to all the various minor ones, and they to him or her. Think how the behaviour of your main character affects the behaviour of the other. To illustrate this, think how different you are with your partner/best friend/child/mother/father/worst colleague. Once you realise that people are chameleons, you will know how your character/s will act with different people in different situations.

Character's Needs.

A principal character in a story should need something to drive the story forward. The need could be long term and incredibly important to them like regaining their sanity or inventing something that will transform the world and their lives or wanting to overcome an addiction, etc. Or it could be a smaller goal like wanting promotion/ wanting to win the lottery, getting one over on the neighbours or trying to get into a house after losing the house keys, etc. Each need can be as intense as the other.

It is important to decide exactly what your character needs. Then work out exactly how far they will go to get it. This second quality I.e. energy, is what drives a story forward. Has your character the energy or skill or desperation to fulfil his goal? This does not have to be mere physical energy; an old character might have a burning mental energy to be able to control the people around him from his bed, even though he is physically frail.

Here are some exercises to ensure that you know these characters well.

7

Character Exercises

1. One of your characters is meeting the other in a place in which s/he is uncomfortable for a reason you decide. Describe in detail how this affects the way s/he acts, thinks and speaks. [One or two pages]

2. Write a scene in which one of your characters struggles with a secret passion. [I.e. the 'passion' doesn't need to be sexual, just secret.] How this person struggles is totally dependent on your person's character traits. [I.e. your character's strengths and flaws.] [One or two pages.]

3. Write a scene to show one thing that your character wants and how s/he is prepared to get it. I.e. this scene should reveal something important about your character - are they manipulative? Arrogant? Fragile? etc. [One or two pages.]

4. A woman called Melanie discovers that Trudie, her best friend, has revealed a secret Melanie had told her never to reveal. This secret involves Melanie's husband and he's the person Trudie has told! How will Melanie feel? What will she do? And what will be the consequences of these actions? [One or two pages.]

N.B. Make sure you give your characters names which will suit them. [If you can't think of any, Google 'names' on the Internet and you'll find hundreds.

Okay, now you know your characters, we are going to let them loose in a plot.

Chapter 2

Genre and Plot

Whatever story you decide to write – consider first what genre you wish to write within. For example: adventure, comedy, romantic, gothic, science- fiction, fantasy, historical, crime, erotic, magic realism, etc. Whatever you decide will influence, and to some extent, limit, the style in which you write and your plot.

Remember, a story can be a playground for the mind; a place where the reader can immerse themselves in an imaginary world full of comedy or drama. A well-constructed story feels absolutely natural to us because we are so familiar with its form. The technique of telling *most* stories should be invisible, allowing the reader to enter the story completely and experience it emotionally.

Look at the following very short story.

There were two goats in the Mojave Desert. They were starving; for days they had found nothing to eat. Then they found a tin of film. The bigger one nuzzled it until the lid came off. The film leader loosened around the spool and the big goat ate a few frames. The little goat tried to butt in and nibble the edge, but the big goat kicked him away and greedily ate the lot. When there was nothing left but the spool, the little goat looked enviously at his big companion and said 'Well, what was it like?'

'It was good,' said the big goat, burping. 'But the book was better.'

This very short comic story has its own conventions – in this world – goats talk. It takes us into this imaginary world and surprises us with its punch line. In the same way, a story has its own world; its own conventions; its own emotional profile and its own way of satisfying our expectations. (Or subverting them.) You will discover the best plotting technique to suit your personality as you develop as a writer. Poets and painters, who move into short story writing, often start with an image which captures their imagination. I'm reminded of the story about the late Harold Pinter who was asked to write the screenplay from John Fowles complex book "The French Lieutenant's Woman". Pinter couldn't start writing until an image came to him in the night; the image of a woman wearing a long green cloak and standing precariously at the end of a slippery quay, while the sea crashed around her. That image opened his imagination; suddenly he had the powerful opening scene in which the beautiful face of Sarah Woodruff, (Meryl Streep) framed by the hood of a green velvet cloak, turns away from the stormy sea to look at Charles Smithson,(Jeremy Irons) and he is lost forever. That image was so powerful that Juniper Films, the production company, used it to publicize the film on posters. If you are a visual writer, perhaps an image will jump-start your plot for you. If not, here are some other methods.

Some of the best short stories focus on one event in someone's life which changes or affects that life in some way. I.e. they reveal a life-changing moment in someone's life that resonates with the reader because it addresses a universal experience.

In fact, Anton Chekhov, the great master of the short story, tried to show us that the precise and subtle evocation of a moment can express a character's whole life. One simple way to do this is to choose a theme like 'betrayal', 'dishonour', 'courage', 'thwarted ambition', 'sacrifice', 'temptation', 'metamorphosis', 'forbidden love', 'a quest' 'honesty' as the starting point of a story. Then use the following list to provide a simple, but effective, blue-print for writing an interesting short story:

1. Start with a character with whom the reader can identify, and from whose point of view the story is told.

2. Confront this character with an urgent problem which he must, but seemingly cannot, solve. [This could be either another character who opposes him or an event which does the same.]

3. To give the story more tension, create more obstacles for your character as he tries to sort out this problem. These obstacles could be internal [created from your character's own flaws] or external [other people or events try to stop him] or a combination of both.

4. Build up these obstacles until it seems impossible for your character to achieve his goal. This escalation makes readers worry about your character's dilemma. Indeed, they should be on the edge of their seats, tense with concern, in case the person you've invented makes a terrible mess of his life.

How you resolve your character's problems at the end of your story is vitally important. The resolution must be believable, but unexpected. Think laterally. What is the most surprising, but credible thing your character can do to resolve her problem? Or, perhaps, you'll discover that you don't want your character to resolve all these problems. [We don't in real life, do we?] If this is what you want, then show us how your character learns some deeper insight about herself and life in general through her acceptance of her defeat.

I can almost hear you thinking – how am I going to create such credible problems in my plot? It's not difficult if you start off with one of the themes I mentioned at the beginning of this chapter. To help you with this plotting process, I'm going to use the theme 'honesty' to create a simple plot like the following:

1. Our main character is a 45 year old working-class man called Michael who is out of work, through no fault of his own. He's a caring man who loves his wife and daughter a great deal.
2. When Michael's angry wife tells him she'll leave him if he doesn't get a job, he's incredibly upset and sends out masses of job applications.
3. He's overjoyed at getting an interview as a school caretaker with a house that comes with the job. However, on the way to the interview he witnesses a woman being knocked down by hit-and-run driver. He's torn between driving off and stopping to help. But as Michael is a good man, he stops and takes her to hospital. [Are you worried about Michael yet? I am.]
4. Michael rings up the school to explain about the accident, but it's too late – it's closed. He's lost the job.
5. Michael drives the injured woman home and tells her about his failed interview and likely divorce. She's appalled by this and rings up the school the next day and speaks to the Head to tell him how Michael stopped to help her.
6. Michael is called for another interview, impresses the Head with his conscientious attitude, and he gets the job.

A satisfying ending, isn't it? But perhaps too neat. What about making your story more complicated? E.g. Michael is so determined to get the job that this time he doesn't stop when he sees the accident. [Although he feels hugely guilty about this because we've created an honest, caring man.] The injured woman doesn't see the real culprit's car, only Michael's which follows it. She memorizes his registration number, thinking he's the one who hit her and the police come after him. Do you see how these complications create a more intriguing plot? Because Michael is honest, the fact that he drives away makes the 'stakes' far higher for him; we know he'll be racked with guilt. Michael is, like all of us, a flawed human being, but we won't want him to be convicted for a crime that he didn't commit because we like him.

Here, I've used conflict to expose character—we learn things about people when they are under stress that we would never find out otherwise. In fact, using conflict is a simple technique for keeping readers interested until you can lead them to whatever you want to reveal.

The Indian writer R.K. Narayan shows a character facing two crises in his short story 'Naga'. When the story begins, a young Indian boy has already lived through the first crisis: he has been forced to face life on his own after his father abandoned him. [Look how J.K. Rowlings used this 'empathy' technique in creating the orphaned Harry Potter.] However, the boy has sufficient knowledge to carry on the family trade of snake-charming, performing with Naga, the cobra, the father has left behind. The story starts at a point close to the second crisis: Naga - old and tired - has become a burden. The boy tries unsuccessfully to rid himself of his dependent by setting him free, only to find that the snake cannot survive on his own. The boy finds that he is incapable of purchasing his own liberty at the price of Naga's life and resumes responsibility for the snake. This is a variation on a theme that often appears in Narayan's stories: an individual wants independence or individuality, but is hampered by forces within his immediate or extended family.

Narayan decided to start his story 'Naga' after the boy's first crisis. This is called the story's 'point of entry'. Deciding on the best 'point of entry' is an important factor in the success of your story. Many writers start a story far too early so the first page is unnecessary preamble.

Remember: make the reader truly care about your main character. If you create empathy and give a character enough conflict, we worry about what's going to happen to him and won't stop reading until the end.

Exercises

1. A useful tool when planning a story is to write a premise. I.e. a sentence or two which describes the story. Think of a story you have enjoyed and write a concise premise of it. (This is not as easy as it sounds as a good premise should cover all the major aspects of the story.)

2. Use one of the themes I've mentioned in this chapter which your characters can illustrate.

3. Now use this idea to write the plot-outline of your story using the above blue-print. Try to start your story as late as possible to achieve the maximum impact. [See next chapter.]

Chapter 3

Openings and Endings

The Point of Entry

'Fiona looked into the mirror, but her reflection had disappeared. Where had she left it this time?'

When submitting your work to an editor, competition judge or publisher, remember - there is only a brief moment to hold their attention so make sure that your 'point of entry' grabs their attention. The opening sentences here would make a good beginning to a fantasy story.

Obviously, hooking your reader with a good 'point of entry' isn't a guarantee to success, but it will make the reader take more notice of the rest of the story. The editor will have a pile of stories to read, so make sure s/he is intrigued by yours because of its arresting opening.

Starting with a surprising, humorous moment is often good hook. Here are the opening lines from my short story called "The Miracle of Breasts".

'Miss Adam-Jones' breasts always walked into the room first; enormous and conical like horizontal traffic cones.'

Or begin your story with immediate conflict.

'His daughter's killer was hiding in the Black Mountains. Kent knew he'd have to climb them; knew that he would never find peace until he had found and killed him.'

I'm already disturbed by both characters from this dark

opening.

Idiosyncratic openings often make lingering hooks. My favourite is the opening sentence of Kafka's "Metamorphosis".

'As Gregor Samsa awoke one morning from uneasy dreams he found himself transformed into a gigantic insect.'

I can still remember this opening after twenty five years because I wanted to know how and why Gregor was transformed.

Another way to draw in the reader is to ask questions which demand the readers' attention.

'How many more days?' Martha asked.
'Four,' Samuel answered without looking at her.
'You can't let him hang!'
'But what can I do? I'm only a farmer.'
'Yes and Nathaniel's only your brother!' She shouted in disgust.

We are immediately confronted with a terrible problem that creates conflict between the characters. This problem piques our curiosity and entices us to carry on reading. We want to know why they're going to hang Nathaniel. Why Samuel isn't prepared to do anything. We also know that this story is not set in the present so the reader is prepared [and expects] details that locate the story in the past.

The Twist Ending
An intriguing twist ending is very satisfying for writer and reader, but be careful to plant enough details throughout the story so that the reader will not only be surprised, but convinced by your ending, and have an emotional engagement with the story. The endings of stories are vitally important. If an ending

lacks impact, readers are going to feel cheated and wonder why they thought the rest of the story was any good.

Unfortunately, many stories that aspire to a twist end fail because the endings are too contrived or illogical. However, in skilful hands the author can lead the reader towards an expected ending, whilst peppering the plot with pieces of information that will plausibly explain a twist ending. If you read Flannery O'Connor's short story "A Good Man Is Hard To Find", you'll see that she uses strong imagery to foreshadow [foretell] the ending to her readers. Next, she mentions one character's murderous tendencies which hint at future events. Later still, she uses images such as a grandmother's dress and a graveyard to further feed our curiosity. Her foreshadowing images are both strong and obscure; so the ending is still surprising. O'Connor uses small events and imagery which hint at things without explaining them clearly until the ending.

Another way to use a 'twist' is to start with the ending and work backwards to the beginning, so we unravel the plot through flashbacks. However, this is complicated and has to be plotted carefully. One method for making this technique easier is to write out the plot as a list. [See Chapter 2.] Then move number 1 to the end. What other numbers do you now have to move to make the plot both intriguing and plausible? However, be careful that you don't strain the structure of your story in an effort to be clever. Remember the best stories only look effortless.

Memorable Endings.
Not all stories have clear resolutions as I mentioned in Chapter 2. Perhaps your story will be far more memorable if you leave readers wondering about the fate of one of your characters. Think of some intriguing open-ended films you've seen. Have you ever gone out of a cinema discussing/arguing with a friend

about what you think will happen to a character? If you can do that in your short story, you've managed to make the character have a life beyond the end of the story. I.e. You've made that character live in your readers' minds. This can be incredibly rewarding for both reader and writer.

Exercises

1. Read as many 'twist' stories as possible.* How do they start? Make a note of them. What technique is the writer using?

2. Practice writing dramatic opening lines using conflict, shock, surprise or humour.

3. Write a 'twist' story using your previous outline.

    a] Use one of your opening lines for the beginning.

    b] Don't forget to 'plant small seeds' along the story's path to intrigue us.

    c] Try to create either an interesting twist or hint at what might happen after the story ends.

* Roald Dahl is a master of the twist ending. [See appendix.]
You can also read 'Twist Stories' on the web-site. www.eastoftheweb.com. [You can also submit stories to this website. Please see UK outlets at the end of the book.]

Chapter 4

Grammar and Great Writing

I know how difficult it is for people to admit that they don't know what an adverb is or how to use apostrophes correctly; that is why I have included this section. It's not difficult to learn the basics of good grammar if you're not bombarded with too much convoluted information. I hope you find the information in this chapter easy to understand and remember.

[The latter part of the chapter will show you how to transform your writing through applying this knowledge.]

PARTS OF SPEECH
Nouns
Nouns [as I'm sure you know] are naming words. They refer to people, places, animals, things or abstract ideas. E.g. 'Carole', 'London', 'cow', 'paper', 'happiness'.

If you want to delve deeper: 'Carole' and 'London' are Proper Nouns because they are specific. [We should use capital letters for Proper Nouns.] 'Cow' and 'paper' are Common Nouns so we use lower case letters. [Except, obviously, at the start of a sentence.] Therefore your name isn't common! Nice thought, isn't it? Abstract ideas like 'happiness' 'courage', 'love' and 'hatred' are Abstract Nouns.

Collective Nouns refer to groups like 'men', 'women', 'people', 'an army of ants', etc.

Verbs
A verb describes an action or a state of being. E.g. 'walking',

'sleeping', 'running', 'thinking', 'living', 'wanting'. These words can be the most powerful Parts Of Speech a writer can use. [See later in the Chapter.]

Adverbs

Adverbs tell you more about the verb. I.e. how, when or how often something is done.

E.g. How. 'Jane ran swiftly.'

When. 'I have to work today.'

How often: 'He gets the train to London every Saturday.'

Try to avoid using 'how' adverbs, that mostly finish in 'ly'. E.g. 'happily', 'cheerfully', 'doggedly' etc, as much as possible in your stories. [More information later in this Chapter.]

Adjectives

An adjective tells you more about a noun. E.g. 'large', 'tiny', 'beautiful', 'amazing', etc. However, be careful to use interesting ones. Readers can't see a 'visual picture' if you write 'The tree was beautiful.' It is far more interesting for them if you show them 'word pictures'.

'The ancient oak's leaf-filled boughs spread out over the meadow like a vibrant, green canopy.' Now I can 'see' the tree. N.B. Do you notice that I've also established exactly what tree I'm writing about? [Details are very important if you want to write vibrant prose. See Chapter 7.]

Pronoun

A pronoun is used to avoid repetition of a proper noun. E.g. 'he', 'she', 'it. 'we', 'they'.

Conjunction

A conjunction joins two words, phrases or sentences together.

E.g. 'and', 'but, 'so, 'because' 'or' 'although'. Be careful not to overuse the word 'and'. Writers often link two dissimilar sentences when two sentences should be used.

Preposition

A preposition links a noun or pronoun to another. E.g. 'to', 'in' 'after' 'under' 'of'. It can have a variety of meanings. E.g.

Direction. 'She is going to the theatre.'
Location. 'It's under the bed.'
Time. 'Thomas left the room after the lesson finished.'
Possession. 'The Government of Great Britain.'

Interjunction

This is added to a sentence to convey emotion. E.g. 'Ouch – that hurt!' 'Hey! Don't do that!'

Active And Passive Voice

Here are examples of the active voice.
1. 'Dr. Pryce will deliver the lecture tomorrow.'
2. 'Scientists will conduct experiments to test this hypothesis.'

Here are the same sentences in the passive voice.
1. 'The lecture tomorrow will be delivered by Dr. Pryce.'
2. 'This hypothesis will be tested by experiments conducted by scientists.'

Can you see how much more direct the active voice is to the passive? And yet, I often read stories that use the passive voice repeatedly. Try to avoid the passive as far as possible as it will make your writing laborious. Make your writing more vigorous by using the active voice.

Tenses

Verb tenses tell readers when events or actions occur in the past, present, or future.

1. The Present Tense

Expresses anything that is happening in the present moment. The present also communicates actions that are ongoing, constant, or habitual. For example:

'I love dancing.'
'Brevity is the soul of wit.'
'Tristan thinks he runs the stock exchange.'

2. The Past Tense

Indicates past events, prior conditions, or completed processes. For example:

'Martin went to the shops every Thursday.'
'Einstein was a genius.'
'Charles Dickens wrote "Great Expectations".'

N.B. Note the use of inverted commas inside inverted commas. [See later.]

3. The Future Tense

Indicates actions or events that will happen in the future. For example:

'I shall go to India next year.'
'Andrew will get his report soon.'

Most writers use the past tense: 'Harry was strolling to work.' [Past Continuous] or Harry strolled to work. [Simple Past] because it feels natural.

Here are two examples written in different tenses.

Present

'On a blisteringly hot day in August, Celia, a repressed woman in her fifties, is driving towards her husband; the man she wants to divorce; the man she hasn't spoken to properly for twenty years. She wonders how she's going to tell him.'

Past

'On a blistering hot day in August, Celia, a repressed woman in her fifties, drove towards her husband; the man she wanted to divorce; the man she hadn't spoken to properly for twenty years. She wondered how she was going to tell him.'

Which version do you prefer? The present tense makes everything more immediate, but there is a danger with using it throughout a story – it is difficult to sustain and easy to lapse into the past. Here's an example of what I mean:

'Celia looks at the darkening sky and worries about an impending storm – the trees started to shake. She runs out into the road as suddenly lightning strikes one of them.'

Do you see the change of tense? 'looks', 'worries' and 'runs' are all in the present tense, then 'started' changes to past. Be careful you don't do the same. Initially, it is easier to use the past tense when writing stories; once you're more experienced, you can enjoy experimenting with tenses.

N.B. The Past Continuous 'Celia is driving the car'' shows that the action is on-going. Use the Simple Past to show a short action. E.g. 'Celia sauntered into the shop.'

The Pluperfect Tense

The Pluperfect Tense is used when you want to move further back into the past, I.e. a flashback, perhaps to show how an event in the past affects someone in the present. However, don't stay in the pluperfect until the flashback ends as it can produce some decidedly stilted writing like this:

'Cecily remembered that Christmas vividly: her mother had been organising the party with her usual skill and attention to detail all day; the table had been heaving with food; the room had been garlanded with flowers and presents for all the family had been placed under the Christmas tree. When the family arrived, everyone had seemed talkative and happy. So when the phone had rung and her mother had answered it, no-one noticed, except Cecily, when her mother had slid down the wall and had collapsed in a heap onto the floor.'

Using the Pluperfect throughout the passage is stilted and laborious. Here's another version.

'Cecily remembered that Christmas vividly: her mother had been organising the party with her usual skill and attention to detail all day; the table was heaving with food; the room garlanded with flowers and presents for all the family were placed under the Christmas tree. When the family arrived, everyone seemed talkative and happy. So when the phone rung and her mother answered it, no-one noticed, except Cecily, when her mother slide down the wall and collapsed into a heap on the floor.'

Did you notice that after the first use of the Pluperfect 'her mother had been organizing,' the Past Tense was used? 'The table was heaving.' You should slide, imperceptibly, from the Pluperfect back into Past Tense when writing about the distant past without the reader being able to notice the time slip.

Transforming Your Writing

Now you know [or have refreshed] some useful grammar, let's use it to its maximum effect.

Strong Verbs

I've mentioned that verbs are powerful Parts of Speech, but people constantly use vague ones. There are a multitude of exciting ones waiting to be used.

Look at these different versions of the same sentence – only the verb has been changed.

1. 'Nigella walked into the room.'
2. 'Nigella bounded into the room.'
3. Nigella crept into the room.'
4. 'Nigella shimmied into the room.'

Do you know anything about Nigella from version 1? No, because I've used a vague verb. But in the other sentences, I've used energetic verbs that suggest something about the state of Nigella's mind to the reader. In 2, she could be excited; in 3, she could be nervous; in 4, she could be feeling sensuous. These verbs are charged with meaning. If a person creeps into the room, two alternatives are placed in a reader's mind: either she's very nervous or she's being very secretive about something; both make the reader interested. If she bounds into the room, she's obviously very energetic or excited. If a woman shimmies into a room, we get the feeling that she's sexy. Look at how altering one verb gives us this subliminal information.

What do we discover about the man in this sentence from the verbs?

'He knocked back his drink, drowned his cigarette in his cup and raced back to his computer to see the results.'

This man is energetic; he wastes no time.

What about this woman?

'She sipped her coffee before studying her nails, then ambled over to the computer and moved papers around.'

She's a time-waster who obviously doesn't want to exhaust herself working. Look at the verbs I've used to slow this woman down!

If you use energetic verbs like 'Martin strides into the meeting', you don't need adverbs like 'Martin walks fast into the meeting.' And vice versa, if you choose more a languid verb like 'amble', you don't need to write 'He walked slowly.'

N.B. Adverbs tend to weaken the impact of sentences.

Use Proper Nouns

I'll rewrite the above sentences to show you how using Proper Nouns will add colour and detail to your writing.

'Jim knocked back the cold dregs of his builder's tea, drowned his roll-up in his chipped mug and raced back to his ancient Acorn Computer.'

Now we know far more about the man – Jim obviously hasn't got much money. He drinks 'dregs' from a 'chipped mug', smokes 'roll-ups' and has an old computer.

In fact, we are painting visual pictures for our reader – these visual details makes writing far more interesting to read.

Look at the difference between these sentences:

1 a. 'Marcus gave his wife a flower.'

1 b. 'Marcus placed one red rose in his wife's hair.'

[In the first sentence Marcus sounds miserly – only one flower! But by being specific – by placing 'one red rose in his wife's hair', Marcus is transformed into a romantic man.]

2 a. '14 year old James lay on the carpet, listening to music.'

2 b. '14 year old James lay on the carpet, totally immersed in the beauty of Bach's "Prelude Number 1".'

We immediately know that James is teenager who adores classical music. I.e. the reader is alerted to the fact that James is an unusual teenager.

By using such details you help the reader form pictures of your characters. Remember to use such details in your stories and you will find people far more interested in publishing them.

Similes and Metaphors

Simile and metaphor can make fiction breathe. A simile [a figure of speech comparing one thing with another] can help readers 'see' what you are describing. E.g.

'Her hair looked like an overstuffed bird's nest.' [See more examples in Chapter 5.]

Metaphor is subtler than simile - it does not compare so much as transform. Metaphors can be contained in one sentence, like 'Albert is one of those little fish that swims under a shark,' which subtly tells us that Albert lives off others, or expanded to thread through an entire story as a central metaphor. E.g. a rainstorm, a mountain or a vivid red dress are images that could be expanded into metaphors for depression, a huge obstacle or danger. [More examples in Chapter 5.]

Mixed Metaphors

Here two dissimilar ideas are incorrectly linked and show sloppy thinking. Avoid sentences like: 'I smell a rat so I'll nip it in the bud.' Or 'Anarchy would bring the Public School System crumbling to its knees.'

Here is a howler which might make you smile:

'Unless somebody can pull a miracle out of the fire, Somerset are cruising into the semi-final.'
Fred Trueman.

Avoid Ambiguity

Ambiguous sentences confuse [and sometimes amuse] the reader. E.g.

'People having relatives buried in this churchyard are requested to keep them in order.'

The sentence should read: 'People should look after their relatives' graves.'

'Mark said his grandfather was still living when he was a child.'

The sentence should read: 'Mark said when he was a child, his grandfather was still alive.'

Of course, George Bush's howlers could fill an entire book. Here is a sprinkling of the incredible malapropisms he has used over many years:

'We cannot let terrorists and rogue nations hold this nation hostile or hold our allies hostile.'

'It will take time to restore chaos and order.'

'They have miscalculated me as a leader.'

Invent Words

Collective nouns are rife for invention. Look at how we can use them:

'A gaggle of geese', 'an army of ants', 'an agenda of tasks', 'a blur of bicycles'. Have you spotted the invented ones? Have fun with language and try to invent some apt ones of your own. [However, be careful that they are apt, if they're not, the reader will be irritated.]

E.g. 'A brace of orthodontists'' suggests a lovely play on the work orthodontists do. While 'a parade of penguins' suggests that they're standing like soldiers.

Try using an established collective noun like 'a gaggle of geese' for a 'gaggle of girls' which suggests they're as noisy as geese. Or 'a vacillation of voters' which suggests a disenchanted view of politics. By inventing new collective nouns, you refresh language in an original way. Try inventing some interesting ones yourself.

Basic Punctuation

The COMMA is used:

To separate words, phrases or clauses. E.g.

'His room was scattered with food, clothes, books and toys.'
'Michael took a long run up, slipped on the path, and landed on his back.'

To mark out a person who is addressed. E.g. 'Don't do that, Sam! You idiot, you've hurt her!'

To mark off a clause or phrase which gives us more information. E.g. 'The girls, who were talking in class, were punished.'

The SEMICOLON is used:
To join two independent clauses or phrases that are closely related in meaning. E.g.

'Neither of us spoke; we simply waited in silence for the other to apologize.'

When clauses or phrases describe a sequence of actions or aspects of the same topic. E.g. 'There was a light wind; a calm sea; a cloudless sky.

To mark off a series of phrases or clauses which contain commas. E.g.

'The furniture consisted of a bed; a number of large, shapeless pillows; four matching wooden chairs with upright backs; and a sideboard that was made in Richmond, Yorkshire.'

[People often use full stops when semi-colons should be used.]

The COLON is used:

To introduce a list. E.g. At Caesar's funeral, Mark Anthony addressed the crowd: 'Friends, Romans, countrymen...'

To express a strong contrast: 'God creates: man destroys.'
To make a pointed connection: 'Marcus was promoted after only two months: his father owned the company.'

To introduce a climax or concluding clause: 'After leaving the church: he became a rock singer.'

Apostrophes

The apostrophe is the most misused punctuation in the English Language and yet there are only two rules for using it:

1. Contractions. When you shorten a word. E.g. 'He shouldn't ', instead of the more formal - 'He should not.'

N.B. You put the apostrophe where the missing letter/s should be. 'Could not' becomes 'couldn't', 'have not' becomes 'haven't'. 'I will' becomes 'I'll', 'could have' becomes 'could've'.

2. Possession. When something belongs to someone. E.g. The cat's tail, Michael's pen, Samantha's perfume, the boy's beret, etc.

Notice where the apostrophe is placed in each phrase.

When you use collective nouns with the possessive, you place the apostrophe after the noun like this: the men's shoes, the women's club, the People's Parliament.

N.B. You place the apostrophe AFTER the S when you have more than one boy with a toy or several girls with high heels. I.e. for plurals.

E.g. The boys' toys; the girls' high heels.

Or, if you have something that belongs to someone with a name that ends with S. E.g. James' desk, Archimedes' principle, Jesus' disciples, etc.

The apostrophe is never used for possessive pronouns like 'yours', 'hers', 'ours', 'theirs' or 'its'. E.g. The cat sat on its tail.' [You only use an apostrophe when you are contracting 'it is' to 'it's'.]

N.B. You never use an apostrophe for plurals like potatoes, tomatoes, lettuces, onions, etc. [Although you will see this mistake constantly on shop signs which always makes me want to rip them up and throw them all over the shop. So far, I've resisted. But for how long? I often ask myself.]

Inverted Commas

These are used for dialogue:

Jane said 'I'm going home.' Note that the inverted comma is placed AFTER the full stop. [Think of inverted commas as 'covering' the dialogue like an umbrella.]

When using quotations:
A famous soliloquy from *Hamlet* begins "To be or not to be". Note that the inverted commas [Double for quotations] are placed BEFORE the full stop if they come at the end of a sentence.

Note: In the past, everyone used double inverted commas for dialogue, but the single inverted comma has now became popular since most people type on computers.

The Exclamation Mark

Expresses some kind of astonishment or sharp outburst. E.g. 'Fire! Fire!'

You can also use it to indicate sarcasm. 'You're a fine one to talk!'
N.B. Don't over-use it as it loses its impact.
The way you present your work is vitally important. If you show

that you know how to use interesting words, write grammatically and use the correct punctuation, you will be stamped with the hallmark of the professional, not the amateur.

Exercise

1. Write a page of vivid writing about a man who is trying to get to break into a house at night, thinking it's empty. It's not – the owners are asleep upstairs. Make your verbs energetic and ensure that you reveal something about the man's state of mind as he breaks into the house.

2. An old woman is lying in bed, thinking of her past life. One memorable thing happened to her that she'll never forget. Use the Pluperfect briefly; then slide into the Past Tense to describe this event or person. [This could make the basis of an interesting short story.]

Chapter 5

Be Creative with Language

'What is life? It is the flash of a firefly in the night. It is the breath of a buffalo in the wintertime. It is the little shadow which runs across the grass and loses itself in the sunset.'
  Crowfoot, Blackfoot warrior and orator, 1890

Isn't the above extract delightful? I love it because it makes me think about what life means for me. Could you sum up what life means for you in the same way? I also love this extract because Crowfoot uses such magical imagery and creative language.

Let's look at how Fishwick and Flaubert explore language in the following two extracts:
  'They were ravished with its loveliness; a warm, soft-voiced spring-green landscape dotted with sassafras and scarlet-colored snakewood, smelling of wild strawberries and hart's tongue.'
  Marshall Fishwick, 'Virginia: A New Look at the Old Dominion', 1959.

'The human language is like a cracked kettle on which we beat out a tune for a dancing bear, when we hope with our music to move the stars.'
  Gustave Flaubert, 'Madame Bovary', 1856.

You might find Flaubert too fanciful but he does make you think, doesn't he? He believed that we are beating out a rhythm of words each time we speak. And he's right, isn't he? Language can be wonderfully rhythmic.
And what do you think of the creative way A.S. Byatt describes

colours in her story called "The Djinn in the Nightingale's Eye"?

'...the fundamental colour of the sky was no longer what they still called sky-blue, but a new sky-green, a pale flat green... something very odd and dimming happened to lemons and oranges, and something more savage and hectic to poppies and pomegranates and ripe chillies.'

Descriptions

Think about how to describe natural events like the seasons. Here are some sentences and phrases that describe winter.

1. After the angry south westerly tempests had finished, the sun shone and the air was like velvet.
2. The winter sky looked as if Turner had painted it with vibrant planes of light.
3. The air was charged with silence and frost.
4. The frost glazed the surface of the snow, till it shone in the red eastern light like polished marble.
5. Withered grass bent, encased in icicles.
6. He saw how the footprints of birds were frozen into semi-permanency along their garden path.
7. The twigs were covered with white fur grown during the night.
8. Above him, Sirius and Orion flashed like stilettos.
9. A blackbird on a dying sycamore tree scanned the garden for food. His crocus-coloured bill opened for a quick trill.

Look at the following examples of describing light.

1. The spider's web stretched across the arch of the window; its radiating threads glistening with reflected light.
2. Her face caught the cold gleam of north-eastern light.
3. The light in her face was soft and creamy like the light

under a buttercup.

4. The lantern's light radiated outwards like the spokes of a wheel.

5. The setting sun gave him a colossal shadow; it stretched eastward until his head rested upon the trunk of an old oak tree thirty feet away.

6. The glow from the candles within the room made the leaves outside dance and created gossamer threads of silver.

7. The bonfire flames towered above us. I turned and saw how shadowed his eye-sockets had become; how the dark wells of his nostrils stood out. I didn't want to look at him anymore: fire had made him grotesque.

As you can see, language can create powerful images if we think carefully about the words we choose when we're writing. If we don't, our language can become stale and boring.

Now let's look at how language can be 'stretched'. I hope you enjoy playing with language after you've read the following:

1. Use nouns as adjectives.
'The sea-sound of a shell.'
'She spat viper words.'

2. Use words in an unusual way.
'The radiant innocence of a star.'
'She was lying flush-red in a sauna.'
'The ammoniac smell of fear.'
'I layered lies around the house.'
'The rough tongue of thirst.'

3. Use the power of metaphors.
'Mondays were always purple for Fiona.'

'A forest carpeted with nightmares.'

'Eyes vivid with violence.'

'She had the tenacity of ivy.'

4. Use similes to intrigue the reader.

'Friends ran out of her life like sand.'

'Her daughter was as delicate as silken thread.'

'Life flattened her like a steam-roller.'

'He's as jumpy as a cricket on crack.'

You will see more interesting examples of playing with language on Nicola Morgan's web-site, so do have a look at it. http://www.nicolamorgan.co.uk/language.php

It also has an interesting section on the condition known as Synaesthesia. Synaesthetes [people who have Synaesthesia] mix senses together. I.e. They can see colours and smell smells when they hear sounds. [To some Synaesthetes, a trumpet sound is scarlet.] Obviously, thinking like a Synaesthete will make your language very creative, but be careful that you use creative language in the correct context. E.g. Don't make a Computer Scientist's dialogue highly creative as it will sound false. [Unless he is a very unusual scientist!] However, in the mouth of a creative character dialogue can 'fly'.

You obviously have an interest in language otherwise you wouldn't be reading this book, so what draws you to words? What world are you trying to create? Draw on your own experiences for they are unique to you. Who else can see the world exactly how you see it? Dig deep into your background and see what you can unearth. You might surprise yourself.

Exercises

1. Write at least 3 examples of your own. [From each

section.]

2. Then write a paragraph which uses language in a way to startle, surprise or seduce the reader.

These are difficult exercises, but they'll make you think carefully about the choice of words you use in your story. Try to use fresh images and creative language.

Chapter 6

Perspective

Who is telling your story? You? One of your major characters or one of your minor characters? More than any other technique, your point of view influences how readers perceive the story you are telling.

First Person Narrative

This is a common technique for creating intimate fiction, but beware – the narrator is not you.

In fiction, the first-person narrator is a character you create. Since you have created him, remember to let him/her speak. [Look back at the check-list I gave you on characterisation.]

Look at the following example:
'Us dress Squeak like she a white woman, only her clothes patch. She got on a starch and iron dress, high heel shoes with scuffs, and an old hat somebody give Shug. Us give her a old pocketbook look like a quilt and a little black bible. Us wash her hair and git all the grease out, then I put it up in two plaits that cross over her head. Us bathe her so clean she smell like a good clean floor.'

In "The Color Purple", Alice Walker has created a quirky voice in her narrator Celie through her distinctive lack of 'proper' grammar. Walker has immersed herself so completely in Celie's world that we see it everything from Celie's perspective. Celie gives Squeak the highest accolade she can find in her narrow, illiterate world – she 'smell like a good, clean floor.' Walker has managed to crawl inside the head of an illiterate black woman and look at the world through her eyes.

The trick of making a first-person narrator's observations authentic is to make sure that the narrator speaks from his own experience, not yours. [Read Walker's powerful extract again.] Think like your narrator and you will start to observe life through his/her eyes.

First Person and Physical Description

'I remember my mother trying to tame my wild red hair when I was five. Tight braids which burned my brain. I used to look up into her cornflower eyes and sun-coloured hair and wonder why I looked like my father.'

Do you see how the relationship between the narrator and her mother is revealed through the simple action of hair braiding? We know that Laura doesn't like the way she looks because her mother obviously doesn't.

A Check List

- Allow your narrator his/her own quirks, prejudices and vocabulary.
- Make sure the narrator's observations fit with his/her world. [Celie sees the world in simplistic terms.]
- When the narrator is a child, simplify the vocabulary, but don't drop all imagery; use imagery applicable to an observant child.
- You could use the plot as part of your description. E.g. 'I was always the last to be chosen for team games because I was so small.'

Third Person Omniscient

Third person narrative is divided into two broad categories:

omniscient [an all-knowing voice] and a third-person-limited point of view.

The omniscient narrator may enter the minds of all the characters. E.g. 'The information Luke gave them terrified Jill, intrigued Martin, but Saul was absolutely disgusted by it.'

Or you can use focused omniscience: 'Luke liked playing games with people: he knew the information he was going to give his family would disturb them, but he really didn't care.'

The omniscient 'eye' may roam all over a story from character to character, place to place, from past to present to future. It may interpret events or merely record them. Unlike the first-person narrator, the omniscient narrator has the entire English language at his disposal. The omniscient narrator may give us a perception of events and also an attitude about those events. Or s/he may be so invisible that we must make our own judgements.

It is up to you to find the voice that fits the story's purpose.

Summary
When determining the point of view for your story, remember your choices. Once you have a good grasp of the limitations and freedoms of various points of view, be sure to match the descriptive style to the point of view you have chosen.

Remember:

- Children see the world differently from adults.
- Old people have a different vocabulary from the young.
- An invisible omniscient narrator adopts a more formal tone than an omniscient narrator who makes his presence felt.
- An educated first-person narrator has a different style of speaking from an uneducated one.

When the point of view is well chosen, the story is seamless, but when the point of view is unclear, the story loses its focus and momentum.

Exercises

1. Describe a car accident in which a driver hits someone. [From the point of view of the driver - one page]

2. Now describe the same event from the point of view of the victim. [This is a fascinating exercise as you have to identity with two opposing viewpoints - one page.]

3. Write the story of Cinderella from the wicked stepmother's point of view. Was she such a bad stepmother or did Cinderella hate her for a secret reason?

4. Choose any story you've read and change the POV. (Point of View.) You'll be amazed at the difference in the story.

Chapter 7

The Importance of Detail

I have already mentioned using detailed verbs and nouns to add spice to your stories, but do you know how to describe the emotions of your character without sounding melodramatic or sentimental? Through using concrete images rather than abstract ones.

Look at the following sentences:

'She was broken hearted. Jon had died and now she was all alone with her tears and aching heart. She felt she would never smile again. She wanted to die too.'

This is turgid prose which doesn't involve us in this woman's feeling of loss because it contains no concrete images. It is all thoughts.

Contrast the above sentences with the following ones:
'That night she lay on their cold bed and reached out into emptiness. She turned to look at a dusty photograph on her bedside table. A man with a hint of grey in his hair was shouting with laughter as he threw a snowball at her. She was almost out of frame as she tried to dodge it. Two middle-aged people with laughter in their eyes. Only six months ago. And now she would never see Jon laugh again.'

These images are real; they allow us to experience what the character is feeling and thus we become involved.

Sometimes it only takes one or two details to spark your

character into life. These 'sparks' are the 'telling details' of fiction; they stretch beyond mere observation to give the readers a richer sense of a character or place.

What do these details suggest?
- a bag-lady with polished shoes
- a pianist with badly chewed nails
- a formally dressed business man wearing psychedelic socks
- a woman who is constantly cleaning
- a quiet man's bedroom covered with photos of sharks

Try to think laterally. Don't go for the obvious interpretations.

Engaging the Senses

Before I became a writer I was an English Lecturer and before that an English Teacher. One hot summer's day, many years ago, I was teaching a class of bored teenagers. Nobody wanted to be inside a stuffy classroom, [especially me!] so I asked them to close their eyes. At first, they looked at me as if I'd lost the plot, so I told them I wanted to take them on a journey through their minds. They were intrigued and closed their eyes. This is what I told them.

'You're walking outside the school and suddenly you smell the most wonderful smell in the world. Breathe in and smell it. What is it? They opened their eyes in interested surprise. Here are only some of the strange and wonderful things they 'smelt': burnt toast, marshmallows, Grannie's apple pie, wood smoke, leaves, tar, home-grown tomatoes, furniture-polish, a leather ball … it went on and on, and soon there was a great discussion about why some people liked certain smells that other people hated. How can tar be a wonderful smell? I asked the boy who'd mentioned it. Because it reminded him of the time his father had taken him for a sailing lesson and the boatyard smelt of tar. Soon they discovered that smells can create powerful images in people's minds from past events. We continued our journey:

'Now, you're walking through a field and the sun is streaming down on you. Listen to the sounds around you. What can you hear and see? At first the details were vague like birds singing; wind blowing, etc, so I asked them to look and listen more carefully. What sort of birds were they listening to? How was the wind blowing? What was the effect of it on the surrounding area? In other words, I wanted details. Soon, they were listening to and looking at 'satin-black ravens cawing'; 'a large rusty tractor bouncing over bumps'; 'a red-faced farmer shouting at a trespasser'; 'a sharp wind slicing the grass like a scythe'. As their descriptions became more and more vivid, they became more and more interested.

Then I moved them onto the sense of touch. I asked them how many of them had played a game when they were small children where they were blind-folded and told to put their hand in a bucket of water. Did they remember the horror of touching something wet and squashy and being told it was an eye? There was a great reaction to that memory. Touch can be as powerful a sense as sight, so please don't forget to use it. I asked the class to describe the differing sensations of touching satin or sand/ tar or water/ talcum powder or grit.

After they had written some very interesting descriptions I asked them to take me on a sensory journey through a wood. I have never seen such enjoyment on teenagers' faces before when they read out their work. They took each one of us on their journey through this wood and we discovered the bitter tang of toadstools; the startle of a nightingale's song; the perfect silence of a secret glade; the kaleidoscope of green fields. In fact, they discovered how to use all their senses and soon their writing became far more vivid as a result.

I have used the same sensory techniques in my writing workshops and students really dig deep in their imaginations when they concentrate on all their senses, not merely on sight. Remember to use as many senses as you can: sight, taste, touch, smell and sound. What your characters smell and hear may be even more important than what they see. A journey down the Amazon River may be great to describe, but what your character smells, hears and touches may be far more important to the overall meaning of the story. [And perhaps, more interesting for the reader.]

Consider this passage.

'Emily leaned down to the soil, breathing its damp, earthy aroma. It reminded her of her childhood, watching her mother gardening. She touched the sunflower's stunted roots, then sat back, confused. In one corner of her balcony lay the withered petals of peonies; her favourite flowers. In another, the rusting remains of carnations, primroses and hyacinths. Nothing grew for her in spite of hours of careful planting. Where were the vibrant colours she saw in her mother's garden? The kaleidoscope of golds and greens and blues? She lifted her head and smelt the early morning traffic snaking below her, choking her lungs, camouflaging the sky. And Emily suddenly realised - the sun had never shone on her.'

Not only is the passage full of sensory details, but it also has a central metaphor for Emily's life - defeat. You can use similar sensory details to explore the central metaphor in your own character's life, making it up-lifting or depressing, depending on the effect you want to create.

Make the small details in your story revealing. Use them as a device through which you introduce your readers to the true nature of your characters.

Exercises

1. Write a short extract to show the changing moods of a child of five.
2. Write a short extract to show the happiness of an old woman.
3. An office is ruled by a young arrogant man. His employees are unhappy. Show the tension in the office, but don't say they are unhappy or that the young man is a tough boss.
4. A business man travels constantly. His wife suspects he's having an affair, but he's not. Show how she discovers the real truth. Try to be original.

[Write one page scenes for 3 & 4]

N.B. Interesting characteristics can reveal something about the person's personality. E.g. If your old woman starts waltzing around the room, it says far more about her personality than if she simply sits in a chair and smiles.

Chapter 8

Anticipation and Fear

Good suspense in stories makes readers so eager to discover how the conflict resolves that they can't read fast enough. We all know that wonderful feeling that comes from being so immersed in a story that the outside world ceases to exist. How do you stop the world from existing? How do you build up credible suspense that makes readers hover on the edge of their seats, desperate to know what's going to happen next? You use two basic principles: anticipation and fear.

Anticipation is a simple concept. In fiction, the secret to anticipation is letting the reader know something bad could happen. We create anticipation by introducing a situation that's fraught with the possibility of danger or risk.

Situation One
A Cabinet Minister is driving down the road, stressed by her job. She's so behind with her work that she takes home some top-secret papers so she can finish an urgent report. [Notice that the 'stakes' have been escalated by making this report 'urgent.'] She's so distracted that she fails to stop at a junction and another driver shouts abuse at her. She apologizes then drives off, still distracted. You know something awful is going to happen, don't you? You're anticipating that she's going to crash and someone will discover she's carrying top-secret documents in her car. What will happen to her, then? How could you stop reading now?

Situation Two
Your main character, a trainee solicitor working in a 15th century building, is sitting at her desk when two men walk past her into

her boss' office without knocking. The door is locked behind them. Why? She thinks. An hour later, she sees them leave, but her boss' door is still closed. She has too much work to worry about this odd event. Of course, the reader hasn't and thinks about it. You have planted the seed of anticipation. Who are the men? Why did they lock the door to her boss' office? What has he done?

Situation 3

A single father is changing the tyre on his car in his garage. When he's tightening the nuts on the wheel, he drops a heavy spanner on his foot. He winces but finishes the job. Just as he's hobbling back into the house, he feels faint, but he's got no time to worry about it as he's got to look after his small son as his wife has died. We have foreshadowed a problem in the future for the father and because he's a single father we start to worry about him.

In each of these situations, the reader knows something bad is going to happen and will try to speculate what that is. But the only way the reader is going to find out is by reading on. That's how effective anticipation is.

However, it is very important not to resolve this anticipation too quickly; let the tension build for pages before you resolve the situation in whatever way you decide. On the other hand, you mustn't string out the anticipation too long or the reader will become irritated. Tease the reader, but don't annoy. Creating good anticipation is a fine balancing act.

While you're creating this anticipation ensure that your narrative is important to the story-line. Don't include unnecessary details which slow the narrative down. Readers don't like writers 'showing off' with unnecessary research that they are determined to put in the story because they like it.

Fear

The second principle of suspense is fear. Fear is inextricably linked with anticipation. Fear occurs after the awful thing has happened, but the outcome hasn't been resolved. Let's take two of the earlier examples and see how fear works.

Situation One

Distracted, the Cabinet Minister doesn't notice the car in front of her has stopped for a red light, and she hits it. She smashes forward and feels confused, then sees the angry driver in the other car coming towards her. He shouts that he's calling the police. She ought to have her licence taken away. What on earth is she going to do? Put the reader in the woman's awful predicament by highlighting the woman's thoughts about what will happen to her career, her marriage and her family if she is discovered.

Situation Two

Work continues in the solicitor's office, but the trainee solicitor's boss doesn't emerge. The trainee is now worried; she walks towards her boss' office and knocks on the door. There's no answer. When she opens the door, she's horrified to find him hanging from an old beam. [Remember it's a Tudor building.] She looks at the papers on his desk which shows he's been embezzling. Then she notices another paper in which he implicates her. Stunned, she's just about to remove the paper when one of the staff walks into the office, sees the body hanging and the trainee trying to remove evidence. The staff member screams and all the other staff rush in. What do you think will happen next?

A character's fears [and the reader's] should increase as the story progresses. The best way to increase fear is to give your main character options at the beginning of the story, then gradually decrease them as the story unfolds. However, make sure you don't escalate the problems so much that the story becomes melodramatic.

Anticipation and fear are vital tools that give interesting tension to a story; they can be woven into even minor conflicts. So don't forget to spice your stories with suspense. You'll be amazed how much more publishable this will make you.

Exercise
Develop a story from Situation 3. Remember to use anticipation and fear by escalating the problems for the poor single father so that you will have your readers desperate to help him.

Chapter 9

Showing Versus Telling

Jane Austin wrote entire novels in the 'telling' style; Philip Roth's novel "Deception" is written entirely in dialogue. I.e. an extended 'show.'

'Showing' is generally thought of as using vivid details and engaging the senses to create a sparkling descriptive picture within the readers' mind, while 'telling' is generally thought of as the absence of vivid detail – the simple description of 'facts'.

Generally speaking, when a story calls for some action, you write a scene. However, this depends on the type of story you are telling. E.g. If you write a crime story about a woman who walks into her local store and discovers a man bludgeoned to death with a hammer – narrative would probably be better. But what if the story is not about the dead man, but about the woman herself? Then you could use a scene to 'show' us something about the woman and how she relates to her husband.

Look at these two different styles.

'On 5th July at 11am, Ellen Parry, [51] walked into her local store and discovered Mr. Herbert Pocket, [48] laying in a pool of blood after being bludgeoned to death. She said she noticed a hammer lying near the victim, then heard a door banging in the distance. She ran into the back of the store and saw a young man in his 20s with spiky hair running away from the scene of the crime....'

Compare the above journalistic narration to this scene:

'I saw something yesterday,' Ellen said to her husband as they sat over breakfast.

'Oh yes,' he mumbled, not looking up from *The Financial Times*.

'A murder. You remember Mr. Pocket from the local store – he was killed yesterday - with a hammer. I saw the killer running away.'

Morris stopped reading briefly to look at his wife. He could never remember her features when he was at the office.

'No, you didn't.'

He got up from the table, flicked some breadcrumbs from his Savile Row suit, and walked to the door. 'I'm late... see you tonight.'

She stared at the paint, peeling down one wall, as the front door banged into the silence.

There's a lot of subtext in this short passage. It reveals a great deal about the husband and wife's 'relationship' without one explicit word being written. I'm sure you noticed the small telling details: the contrast between Morris' expensive suit and the peeling paint in the kitchen reveal that Morris isn't interested in his home or his wife. The appalling gulf between them is further highlighted by this simple statement: 'He could never remember her features when he was at the office.' These small details also make us empathetic to his poor wife's predicament in being married to such a self-centred man.

Here are some more examples of the difference between showing and telling.

Example I

Told: The Bakers were poor.

Shown: 'Daniel Baker looked at the pile of bills in front of him on the kitchen table. What the hell was he going to do? He couldn't make the figures add up. Perhaps he could just pay for the rent and forget about the heating bill? Then he remembered what had happened last year: the oil company refused to deliver any oil and they had all shivered under threadbare blankets for three months. The first snow was due soon. He couldn't risk the health of his family again.'

The 'shown' example never uses the word 'poor', but we have no doubt that the Baker family is exactly that. That's because the details show that Daniel has to stretch his budget; he doesn't have enough to cover everything so he has to make choices. Through the choices he is forced to make we get an idea of the level his poverty. We know he doesn't own his own house, but rents. We know that his money troubles have been going on for at least a year because he had problems last winter. We also know that winter is coming again, although we haven't been told it directly. The snow is a detail that shows us the relentlessness of the seasons.

[Of course what one person thinks is poverty, another might not. Some people might feel poor if they can't go on holiday; for others, it means not eating. For a family in Nigeria, Daniel's poverty might represent wealth.]

Example 2
Told: Flora ate the dessert.

Shown: 'Flora tasted the seduction of strawberries, the silkiness of vanilla and the ice-green sliver of lime.'

The difference: The word 'dessert' is vague, while the words in the 'shown' example, engage our senses with imagery and a startling play on words. Each small detail makes us re-evaluate what food really is.

The best descriptions should combine 'showing' what a person/place is like and 'telling' us. In its simplest form: 'showing' can be thought of as 'scene' and 'telling' as 'narrative'. Scenes are most effective when you are trying to reveal the complex interplay between characters (or a character and himself), while narrative is most effective when giving the reader background information about a character or place.

Exercise

1. Reread some favourite stories and identify the passages that tell, the ones that show, and the ones that combine the two.
2. Take two of your 'memorable' characters and write about them using a combination of 'showing and 'telling'. Try to make them linger in our imagination.

Chapter 10

Movement and Pace

Without forward movement, even good characters can find themselves in dull stories. Characters must do something: interact with people, with places, with their own emotions. Make sure your character gets from point A to point B, [however circuitous the route] by the end of your story.

Think about what your character does. Make sure that she reveals herself through her words and deeds. Good stories are often psychological in nature I.e. character-driven as opposed to plot-driven. Even so, when writers are asked what their story is about they relate the plot: a husband and wife lose their child at an airport; a biker runs over a woman; a man discovers his wife is leaving him. This physical information is what the story is 'about.'

However, what turns the plot into a story is the emotional/psychological information that we convey to the reader. I.e. the character's inner landscape: a woman discovers the melancholy of her marriage; a man discovers his hatred of women; a child discovers his separateness from his parents. It is these emotional discoveries that make stories interesting, horrifying, beautiful or compelling.

Make your story move on two levels: physical and emotional. Here is an example of what I mean.

Physical Movement
1. In a department store, a middle-aged woman, Rebecca, sees a diamond ring which sparkles in the sunlight. She

      steals it.

2. One morning, her husband Harry tells her that a young man in his 20s has been accused of stealing the ring.

3. She gets up and washes the dishes.

4. She discovers that the young man has gone to prison.

5. The husband discovers his wife's hoard.

6. He gets rid of the rings.

Emotional Movement

1. A wealthy woman, who has been ignored by her husband for years, has developed an addiction for stealing engagement rings – symbols of romance.

2. When she returns home we discover that she has hundreds of similar rings casually thrown in a drawer – waiting to be discovered.

3. She is upset when her husband tells her a young man has been accused of stealing rings, but thinks he will be acquitted.

4. However, when she discovers that the man has gone to prison, she is horrified, but too frightened of the consequences to go to the police. Her health deteriorates dramatically and she lives on tranquillizers.

5. She tries to tell her husband many times about her stealing, but he is always too preoccupied by his work to listen to her.

6. However, one day Harry opens his wife's drawer and is stunned to discover the rings. As he is an Inspector of Police, he obviously has far too much to lose if he reveals what his wife has done. So one night he takes the rings and throws them in a local lake.

The story ends as the story began. His wife steals another ring because the husband never acknowledges his wife's problems.

Do you see how plot and character are inextricably linked? The physical content should move with the emotional. One can exist without the other, but both are enriched by the other's presence. Can you see how the emotional stakes in the story have been raised by making Harry a Police Inspector? If he was out of work, for example, the discovery of the stolen rings would not have such an impact.

Pace

When you are writing a story you are really manipulating time. So deciding the length of time you're covering in your story is important. Think whether the events in your story happen in a day or a week or a year or even longer. Obviously if you are covering a longer span of time, you will use more narrative and less scenes and vice versa. If you want dramatic action you will need to use scenes. It is important that you allow the dramatic moments to happen 'on stage.' I.e. Let the reader see the crisis that happens in your character's life unfold before him. This increases the pace of the story and sucks the reader in.

The pace of a story should also be controlled by the physical and emotional content. Therefore, in the above story, when Harry relates that a man has been arrested, the pace could be leisurely. However, the pace should quicken dramatically when Rebecca discovers that the same man has actually been convicted and is going to prison. In this way, her agitation and panic are illustrated subtly to the reader. [A useful technique to quicken pace is to use short, staccato sentences and vice versa when you wish to create a slower one.]

Flash-Backs

A flashback is a narrative passage that takes us to the past before your story is set. It should reveal something about a character that we didn't know before that explains his motivation, by showing, not telling. You could use a flashback to a character's childhood to show the reader why he thinks and acts the way he does. [This technique also overcomes a reader's incredulity if a character acts [seemingly] out of character. E.g. A man, who has always been gentle, sees another man hit a woman in a park and he reacts violently by beating the man up. Then we flashback to his childhood to a scene where his father is hitting his mother and he's too young to protect her. We now understand why he acts so violently.

In Charles Dickens' "A Christmas Carol" we see Scrooge as a boy in flashback and feel sorry for him. The same technique is used with the character of Anders in the story "Bullet in the Brain" by Tobias Wolff. Anders is portrayed as especially unsympathetic. The story is told in the present tense, except for a flashback in expository prose that enumerates all the events in Anders' life that flash through his brain as a bullet goes through his head during a bank robbery.

The key to using a flashback is relevance. If you use a flashback which doesn't enrich the story by its insight, don't use it as it will slow the story down. Also ensure that the flashback isn't too lengthy. Many years ago I was judging a short story competition and one story contained such lengthy flashbacks that the focus of the story was completely lost. Page after page was related in flashback, then just as I was becoming used to being in the past, the writer jarred me into the present. Then when I was used to being in the present, he jarred me back into the past again. I had to keep rereading the story to make sense of it. Needless to say, the writer wasn't short-listed. Readers want to read stories which capture their attention, not irritate them.

If you don't want to use a flashback, you could give us some vital information about the past through dialogue. E.g. a man speaks to his mother about his father's aggression.

'But why was Dad always shouting at me?' Paul asked with pain in his voice. 'I was only a child. I'll never forgive him.'

'He wasn't shouting at you, he was shouting at me,' his mother whispered. 'It was nothing to do with you. It was me he hated.'

Paul looked at the sorrow in his mother's face and realised that he didn't really know anything about his parents at all.

In this extract I'm focusing on how the father's treatment of his son in the past impacts on the relationship he has with his mother in the present. It is also intriguing for the reader. Why was the father shouting at the boy, not the mother? Here I have used subtext. There is a lot more going on in the relationship between parents and son than I've revealed in the actual prose. Be economical with your words. Imply what you can about the character or situation without being obvious.

Foreshadowing

Remember the previous chapter about anticipation?

Foreshadowing is the anticipation of conflict. E.g.

1. 'Yesterday morning a car ran Mrs. Johnson over and killed her. A witness said she thought the car belonged to Mr. Johnson.'
2. 'Looking back now, I realise all my problems stem from my parent's divorce.'
3. 'The boy slung a rifle over his shoulder as he ran out to the school bus.'

All these openings intrigue us and make us ask questions.

1. Did Mr. Johnson really kill his wife? And if so, why?
2. What are the unseen narrator's problems?
3. How is a boy allowed on a school bus with a rifle? What is he going to do with it?

Foreshadowing creates suspense by suggesting something that WILL happen. E.g.

'Susan had no idea when she paid £8 for the afternoon matinee that she had just made one of the biggest mistakes of her life. She should have stayed home that day.'

We don't know what calamity is about to befall Susan, but we know that something is and we look forward to knowing what it was. [Terrible, but true.]

Edgar Allan Poe used foreshadowing a great deal in his stories to create tension. Look at the opening of "The Cask of the Amontillado":

'The thousand injuries of Fortunato I had borne as I best could; but when he ventured upon insult, I vowed revenge.'

How could poor old Fortunato live happily after that comment?

Starting at the End.
'Thirty-year-old James Sullivan's body lay on the carpet; his blood seeping into its yellow fibres from the knife-wound in his back.'

From this opening I've created, I would have to go back to the beginning of the story and explore who James is, why he was murdered and who did it. [If you've ever watched the series "Columbo" on T.V. you'll recognise this technique is the one the screenwriter used.]

You can also employ minor characters to foreshadow the actions of the major characters. However, always remember, if you plant an intriguing detail through foreshadowing, make sure you reveal exactly what it means by the end of the story or the reader will feel cheated.

Exercises
1. Use the list in this chapter to write out the physical movement in your story.
2. Do the same for the emotional movement. How are they linked?
3. Now use foreshadowing to intrigue or surprise the reader.

Chapter 11

How To Create Great Dialogue

Dialogue is an extremely powerful tool in fiction but should be used with care; characters need to *sound* real, but real people do not speak in complete, formal sentences. Listen on a train the next time you go on one and listen to the way people actually speak. They interrupt each other or change the conversation's direction. [We all know the feeling of not being listened to!] Listen to the slang people use. Remember how young people scatter the word 'like' throughout their conversation. E.g. I was like walking down the road.' This marks their age. Have you ever heard an older person speak this way? The way people use words also marks where they come from. The Welsh often end sentences with a question like this. 'You won't guess who I saw yesterday, will you?' The Irish use idioms like 'to be sure.' However, be careful you don't overdo idioms or you could be creating a stereotypical person.

Remember also that every word your characters say needs to fit a specific purpose. Simply moving the story forward isn't enough. It must also reveal nuances of their character, reveal a tiny fragment of their back-story, and suggest their relationship to the character they're speaking with.

Listen in on conversations and you'll discover that there is often one who leads and one who follows. The next time you hear two individuals conversing, take careful note: who has the upper hand? How is this shown? Through tone of voice or through body language, or something else entirely? And, if this is the case, how would you describe it on paper?

A Cautionary Tale

Try not to make eye contact with people whose words you want to steal or you might become a victim of your own success. To illustrate this point, I'll tell you about a journey I had a couple of years ago when travelling by train from Charing Cross to Tunbridge Wells. I was happily rereading Michael Ondaatje's "An English Patient" when a conversation between two women on seats in front of me filtered through my concentration. It went something like this:

> Woman 1: 'Well, I 'ad to 'it 'im, didn't I?'
> Woman 2: 'Why?'
> Woman 1: 'Ain't you listenin'? Told you. I 'ad to 'it 'im.'
> Woman 2: 'Cos?'
> Woman 1: 'You mental or what?'
> Woman 2: 'Naw!'
> Woman 2: 'Cos 'e was 'ittin' me, wasn't 'e?'

I started writing down their words faster and faster when suddenly, Woman 1 got up from her seat and leaned over me.

'What you doin'? You a nark?' She bellowed.

I cringed as the woman, who held all the fire of Boudicca, glared at me. I said I was just interested in words.

'Words! What f.... words you interested in?'

'Oh, any old words, really,' I said lamely as I tried getting up.

'You're a gabby gaffer, ain't you?' she yelled as she pushed me down in my seat, tore my notebook out of my hands and ripped it into shreds in front of me.

Everyone in the compartment pretended to be fascinated by their shoes or fingers or newspapers. As I said: never make eye contact with people whose words you want to steal. They might do things to you that you wish they wouldn't.

However, it also taught me another important lesson: authentic dialogue is important to your success as a writer.

Monologues

Monologues are a great way of getting into a character's head and looking out at the world through their eyes. If you're finding it difficult to 'pin down' your characters, try letting them write about their life and you might discover something interesting about them you never suspected.

Here is a monologue I've written about a man who works at an unusual place. I hope you enjoy it.

Tristan

"Why are you doing this? I ask myself for the hundredth time as I try to brush my teeth with three flat bristles. Pay's lousy. Food's lousy. Inmates are *really* lousy. Yesterday, I leant over Harry the Hatchet [I've never asked] who now calls himself Bob de Niro, [that's what happens when you tell them to be imaginative] and some little buggers buried themselves in my hair. They must have been at it all night because I can see my hair moving in the mirror.

Harry aka Bob has been excited all week. He's just discovered words and wrote LIFERS HAV RITS TO! LET ME AUT YER BASTADS! on his cell wall. He beamed when I told him that his punctuation would really impress the Governor. We're working on his spelling and vocabulary so he can write letters to his Missus. [I realise that as his vocabulary expands, mine is shrinking.]

'Love letters?' I asked naively. He looked at me as if I'd just given him ringworm.

'Yer seen my Missus?'

'No,' I said. 'You haven't any photos.'

'There's a reason for that,' he said, snorting with laughter, before punching me playfully on my right shoulder and slamming me into the cell door. Thank God, I'm left handed. The doctor at A & E said he'd seen far worse dislocations than mine and told me to stop whining.

'What about the pain?' I whimpered.

'That's the body's way of warning you,' he said enigmatically as he walked off.

'Warning me of what?' I shouted after him, but got no response.

'I fought in the Second World War for blokes like that doctor,' an old man said proudly as I staggered towards the door.

'You shouldn't have bloody bothered!' I shouted just before the automatic door clipped my shoulder. My screams echoed down the hospital corridor.

'Pansy!' The old man shouted back.

I thought of taking him on, but had to catch the bus home. Of course, no prison staff to pick me up. So here I am, staring into my bathroom mirror, contemplating my future with a head full of lice, a dislocated shoulder and in chronic pain. I don't understand what went wrong. At 21 the world was my oyster. [Oh, God, I'm starting to use clichés and I've got a first class degree in English!] At 21 I could have taken on the world like tenderloin toughie Jimmy Cagney in 'Angel with Dirty Faces', so how did I end up being fifty-years-old and working in a prison as a creative writing tutor? No, shouldn't that be Creative Writing Tutor? [Dear God - why am I bothering about Proper Nouns when I'm teaching lifers?] My mother always said that compassion would get the ... what did she say? I think I'm getting Alzheimer's as well as a dislocated shoulder. Oh, no! I've just written an ambiguous statement and I keep telling the lifers about the problems ambiguity causes in Law Courts. What's happening to me? Where's the creative clarity I had at University when I called a spade a cunning contraption with a heavy handle and a biting blade that could be teased into the terra firma with a flat foot?

I told the Governor I needed time off work because of my dislocated shoulder and within seconds, his face was a colour-copy of the prison walls – gravel-grey.

'What will happen to the prison if you don't teach Harold Baldwin to write letters?' He whispered, clenching his fists over his desk for support. I couldn't help noticing the interesting contrast in colour between his white knuckles and the walls. I'm always telling the lifers they should observe interesting details in the prison to help them paint creative word pictures in their letters to their families. Unfortunately, their superior observational skills created a riot three days ago: the lifers started observing all the wheeling and dealing going on in their 'patches'. The next day, Frankie-Four-Fists-McKleane went to the library to 'observe' words in a large book called "Find An Interesting Word " and observed a collection of knives, a detailed map of the prison and an escape route hidden inside the space where the pages should have been. He wrote about his surprising findings in a letter to his Missus, telling her that some of the lifers had practised writing their names on the map. When the Governor called me in to decipher Frankie's letter, I felt honour-bound to grass those involved, thinking they'd be moved to another prison. They weren't. The escape committee comes out of solitary in two weeks and since knowing this Edgar-Allan-Poe-piece-of- information, I've been having surreal dreams about being chopped into pieces, squeezed through a small mincer, covered with an intestinal lining and being offered up as the Free Range Succulent Sausages Option in the prison canteen.

When I told the Governor with counterfeit-nonchalance that I didn't care a toss what would happen to the prison if I didn't teach Harold Baldwin to write letters as I didn't know who Harold Baldwin was, his hands developed a strange irregular tremor as if they were doing the tango without any lessons. At that moment, I knew that the stress of the job was affecting him big time.

'Of course you know Harold Baldwin - you've been teaching him to read for six months.' He squeaked in such a high falsetto that I wondered if an unseen lifer had suddenly crept in and strapped gaffer tape around his testicles.

I told him he must have mixed up his files because I'd never seen Harold Baldwin, let alone taught him.

'Have you heard of Harry the Hatchet? Have you heard of Bob de Niro?' he squeaked repetitively. [And there's me telling the lifers not to be repetitive in their letters as it could cause monumental problems with sustaining their families' interest.]

His falsetto voice was setting up an appalling vibration in my head, which, coupled with the searing pain in my shoulder, almost caused me to faint. But I haven't worked with lifers for nothing. Ignoring the agony, I answered him soothingly.

'Yes, I've heard of Bob de Niro, Governor. I've been trying to teach him to read for six months.'

'Well, Bob de Niro is Harry the Hatchet is Harold Baldwin. And do you know what he did?'

I said I didn't want to know, but he insisted on telling me in spite of my agonising pain.

'He took a hatchet and chopped his mother-in-law into pieces.'

The Governor stared at me, obviously trying to gauge my reaction as I pondered on the possibility of being able to chop a body into pieces. In my lucid moments, I knew my dreams were only wild fantasies. You'd have to be a surgeon to be able to hack through all the bones, wouldn't you? The hairs on the back of my hands suddenly shot up; the prison could be filled with an operating theatre of surgeons for all I knew.

'Look, Tristan... we're all in this together,' the Governor continued, lowering his voice an octave and projecting one of his facsimile smiles onto my face. The change to over-familiar-clichéd gear didn't do it for me. 'You can't take time off. I've got to think of the welfare of my staff. What's going to happen to everyone after Harold/Harry/Bob runs rampant through the prison?'

Imagination is a double-edged sword; I knew exactly what would happen if I didn't teach Harold/Harry/Bob: the prison would look like an abattoir. So tomorrow, I've got to teach this woolly mammoth of a man; a mammoth who hasn't yet mastered the complications of the alphabet, how to write letters home to a family full of Neanderthals.

As I walked home in the deary dark accompanied only by head-lice and intense pain, my mother's prophetic words seared my brain: 'Darling – there *really* are more useful subjects than English.'

Oh, Mummy - why didn't I listen?

Description and Dialogue

Description and dialogue are usually discussed as entirely separate techniques. Description through dialogue is a challenge, but as characters view people/ events/ situations differently, the kind of dialogue they use tells us a great deal about them.

Consider the following about Darrel; a young man who works very long hours. He meets a young woman called Nicola in a pub on his day off.

'You work nights?' Nicola said, surprised.

'I'm a nurse,' Darrel answered. 'Someone has to look after the patients at night.'

Nicola thought about this. 'I'd hate working at night. It must be kind of creepy being in a ward in the dark.'

'No, it's marvellous,' Darrel said. 'The solitude, the pristine quiet, the strange shapes of the hospital equipment, the patients, lying like sentries in their beds.'

This writer doesn't know Darrel's character, does s/he? Would a nurse speak so artificially? What do you think he'd notice about the ward at night? And what would that tell us about his personality?

Exercise

Rewrite Darrel and Nicola's dialogue so we learn something more interesting about their personalities.

Dialogue and Body Language

Your protagonist may have a favourite saying/swear word/exclamation that is his trademark. He may resort to clichés or use proverbs. However, while he is talking, he will seldom remain still. He will often use body language to indicate his frame of mind. He may make faces, move his body awkwardly or speak in a particular tone of voice.

Consider this example:

'So, what did you think of Roger?'

Sally didn't answer. She knew what was coming.

'Did you like him?' Matthew toyed with a spoon, turning it over and over in his hands.

'I... liked him. He seemed pleasant enough.' She couldn't look at her husband's eyes as he sat, watching her.

'Seemed to get on with him very well at the party. You were positively animated in fact.'

'I was talking about the children ... you know ... telling him how well they were getting on at school.'

'Really? Obviously Roger finds children very funny.'

'What?'

'You were both laughing so much. Everyone noticed.'

'What are you talking about?' Sally felt her stomach tightening.

'The night of the party. The night you ignored me.' He dropped his spoon onto the table.

'You're always accusing me! Always doubting me! I'm tired of your paranoia! If you don't stop it, I'm leaving you!'

Matthew suddenly rushed up and hugged her. 'Oh, darling - I'm sorry.' She shivered as he kissed the back of her neck. 'I love you so much, I'm frightened of losing you ... I know I shouldn't doubt you.'

Oh yes, you should, she thought, then smiled at him with all the innocence of their children in her eyes.'

[Note the way the characters interact; how Matthew and Sally's body language demonstrate their tension, how it characterizes them and shows the rapid reversal of their moods.] But don't you think Sally's dialogue is a little melodramatic?

Dialogue and Style

We talk to impart information, to ask questions, to express emotion or opinion, to influence or persuade, to discover things, to give advice, or just to hear the sound of our own voices.

It is important that opportunities for using dialogue are not squandered - always make sure that no word is wasted, and that it has a purpose in the story, in terms of the above.

Writers with a 'good ear' for dialogue will be able to write conversations in such a way that the reader will understand the sub-text. I.e. the thing that the speaker is really speaking about or hinting at. Also, it will not be necessary, in a good piece of dialogue, to describe how the writer is delivering the speech. For instance, ''I'm leaving!' she said impatiently,' could be written as 'I've had it! I'm off!' We don't need the adverb, 'impatiently'.

Practice makes perfect with this skill, and leaving out some adverbs (such as 'impatiently') is a good way of getting there.

Setting out your dialogue is simple. When a character speaks, you will need a new line to show that. For a reply or comment from another character, use another new line.

For instance:

'She's real bitch.' Julia said before turning and seeing Laura standing in the doorway. 'Oh God - I didn't realise you were here.' The colour drained away from her face.

'Obviously not, but at least I've learned something - I'm useless at choosing true friends.' Laura answered, before striding off.

If you want to continue with a description of each character's expression or movements after they speak, do so, and then if they speak again, begin the next piece of dialogue on the same line, for continuity.

Everyone's writing style is their own, and it is this which gives your work its distinctive voice. The most impressive and stylish writing is that which reads naturally. When a complex word is used, it should be used appropriately, without any sense of a thesaurus lurking in the background. But sometimes a banal word will come as a surprise to the reader and could demonstrate something about a character's state of mind. Good writers choose their vocabulary naturally: they write with economy and precision - and in time, with pruning and confidence, your own style will develop in this way.

Many modern writers are influenced by the journalistic, staccato style of Ernest Hemingway. Hemingway used short, repetitive sentences that sounded like natural speech, and his language was direct and uncluttered. Some find it rather mannered today, but studying Hemingway's style is never wasted.

I think the following words Hemingway wrote might be the shortest, most poignant story in the world.

'For Sale. Baby Shoes. Never Worn.'

That's how packed Hemingway's prose could be.

In complete contrast, there is the lyrical, poetic prose of writers like D H Lawrence. Read a passage from *Sons and Lovers*, or *The Rainbow*, to get a flavour of this kind of writing. Then look at the work of Virginia Woolf or James Joyce, for the completely different 'stream-of-consciousness', where ideas and thoughts pour forth *seemingly* as they occur.

Try not to use clichés in your writing unless it is used for dialogue. [They can give a natural feel to conversations sometimes.] Find a way of describing that is not hackneyed or re-hashed, but is your character's personal response.

What is Great Dialogue?

Checklist

1) When a character says something in a fresh, clever way.
2) When characters express a unique sense of humour.
3) When the words are so crisply suited to each individual character in the story we can tell who's speaking without looking at the character's name.
4) Dialogue can serve to show us the class, attitudes, sex, prejudices, nationality, state of mind, honesty, education and ambition of a character, in one sentence. E.g. 'Nickin' stuff is the only way me and the missus survive in this shitty world.'
5) When it helps move the story on. E.g. ' There's something I ought to tell you. I'm going to live in Italy with Julian next week.'
6) It can be used to sum up things that have gone before, or to fill in details about a character's past, as well as, or

instead of, the narrator describing them. This gives an authentic 'first-person' feel to a piece of information, which we can judge the truth of for ourselves, as we read. Therefore there is not such an 'authorial' tone to the writing, with the author as omnipotent and all-knowing. The reader has more space to make up his or her own mind about things.

Exercises

1. Write a scene [a page] with two characters in conflict and use those characters' body language to show what they are feeling.

2. Rewrite the above scene with Sally and Matthew to make their dialogue more interesting and believable.

Chapter 12

Location

The location of your story is not merely the physical backdrop of the tale, but may also include the historical background and cultural attitudes of a given place and time, the mood of an era, and include details such as how people speak. Consider your location carefully as it will influence the style in which you tell your story.

For example: "Robinson Crusoe" – how profoundly different Defoe's book would have been if the author had chosen another setting – perhaps the Arctic! And what about the 20th century book "Captain Corelli's Mandolin"? Since Louis de Bernieres set his book in Cephallonia, a Greek Island, during the Second World War, the influence of this island's history and people becomes an integral part of the book. Indeed, de Bernieres' book can be seen as a portrait of an island and its people.

Your chosen location does more than provide a framework within which the story is told; it makes certain things possible, and others impossible. Again, if we look at "Captain Corelli's Mandolin", the fact that it is set in Greece means that de Bernieres can explore the notion of honour – the fact that if Pelagia breaks off her betrothal to Mandras, not only will she be dishonoured, but so too will her fiancé Mandras, his mother, and her father! A Greek concept which would be impossible to set in present day Britain and one which gives so much piquancy and intensity to the love affair between Pelagia and Antonio Corelli.

Compare these two extracts:

"Word Games"

'The sun was shining on the mock Tudor façade of the library as Alice walked carefully up the steps and opened the large oak door. It slanted across the black and white tiled corridor, almost touching the double doors at the end of it. Almost reaching into the library. Alice opened the doors onto the dusky Victorian room and looked around. Perfect. All the books were aligned exactly as she had left them last night. The cleaners had obviously read her little note, reminding them to place any books, accidentally knocked off the shelves, in the correct Dewy-Decimal position.'

The description of the library also tells us about Alice, doesn't it? Alice is a perfectionist; she finds pleasure from the fact that the books are aligned in perfectly positioned rows. As the story progresses, I reveal, in subtle ways, the reason why Alice likes to be in control of things. It's a disturbing tale.

"The Vanishing Point of Puzzles"

'Phil and I consoled ourselves by walking around the ruins of Scotney Castle. All that remained of this time-worn 14th century building was a massive round tower and a crumpling gatehouse. But it was beautiful, surrounded by Japanese maple trees. Each day we sat by the water-lilied moat and studied the refracted reeds in the water; the cobwebbed light on old medieval stones; the oblique angles in the tower. And as I taught Phil how to develop an eye for perspective, I learned to see what he might become.'

Here, I've used a location to reflect the narrator's life: Fiona is a painter with a ruined marriage, but she can still see the beauty of her future with her son.

N.B. Note how I've used differing points of view: "Word Games" is narrated in the 3rd person by an unseen narrator, whilst "The Vanishing Point of Puzzles" uses the more intimate

1st person perspective.

The science fiction writer, Ray Bradbury often got an idea for a story by thinking of a place. His story "The Playground" uses location to explore the trauma of Charles Underhill's childhood. Underhill is a widower who wants to protect his young son Jim from the horrors of a playground they pass daily which brings back the anguish of Underhill's own childhood. For Underhill, the playground, like childhood itself, is a nightmare of torment and vulnerability. He fears that his sensitive son will be destroyed there, just as he nearly was, so many years ago.

Are you hooked by underlying conflict and emotional resonance in the story? Do you want to know what happens to Underhill and his son? I do.

Location and Character

Have you thought about how location affects people? How differently a child being bought up in the Swiss Alps thinks [and therefore acts] to a child being brought up in a green Welsh valley. Landscape influences people a great deal. The Welsh writer, Dylan Thomas, was deeply influenced by being brought up in Swansea, a seaside town of Wales,[now a city] opposite Cwmdonkin Park [where he wrote a lot of his poetry] and being able to see Swansea Bay from his bedroom window. So many of his stories feature the park and the sea. Can you imagine how different his stories would have been if he had been born in Africa?

You will, perhaps, want to use your own experiences of life in your stories, but always remember the Internet; it is an incredibly useful research tool and can be used to explore new, interesting locations.

Location and Horror

The location in "The Cask of the Amontillado" by Edgar Allan Poe* plays an important role in creating tension and horror. Poe sets this horror story at carnival time; (the irony of which should not escape us). To deepen the horror, [forgive the pun] Poe locates his story in catacombs that have walls made from human remains. The story is told from the perspective of Montresor who leads his so-called friend Fortunato through the vaults down the long and winding staircase to the 'damp grounds' of the catacombs of the Montresors. Montresor seeks revenge for an unspecified insult. He opens a bottle of wine and Poe uses more irony by having Fortunato drinking to 'the buried that repose around us' and the devious Montresor drinking to his friend's 'long life'. Poe describes the setting in detail – the men walk past 'long walls of piled skeletons, with casks and puncheons inter-mingling, into the inmost recesses of the catacombs' to intensify the dark atmosphere.

The greatest use of irony comes when Montresor says he is a member of the masons. Fortunato believes he means he's a fellow member of the society, but, in fact, Montresor is using the term 'mason' literally – he is going to become a bricklayer who is about to brick Fortunato in for all eternity. Poe uses this conversation to foreshadow the evil that Montresor will soon perpetuate. He deepens the horror by having Montresor carefully construct each row of stone in spite of the desperate pleas from Fortunato. The last line of the story 'In pace requiescat' is exquisitely ironic as it means 'may he rest in peace'. The poor man is being walled in alive! This is an apt location for a horrifying story about revenge and death.

* Poe's story can be read at the end of the book.

Exercises

1. Look at the previous chapter where Sally and Matthew are speaking. Do you know what's missing from this extract? Location. Where are they when they are speaking? In their bedroom? A restaurant? A friend's house? The Caribbean? Can you see how different their dialogue would become if you placed them in a restaurant full of people or had them climbing a mountain?

2. Rewrite the extract from Chapter 8 and place them in a busy restaurant where people might be listening to their conversation. Give descriptions of the people and the restaurant which will impact on their conversation.

3. After reading Poe's story, try to create a horror story, full of ominous suspense, like Poe's by choosing a suitable location and devising a dark plot.

Chapter 13

Description and Style

Your style as a writer comes from making choices: from your genre; your point of view; your sentence length; your setting, through to your choice of words. As you revise the first drafts of a story you should be asking yourself certain questions:

- Is the main character the right one?
- Am I using the best point of view?
- Does my structure enhance or hinder the story's progress?
- Should I change tense?
- Do I need more scenes and less narrative?
- Are the paragraphs too long/too short/too similar?

These questions will force you to re-evaluate what you've written. Do you always write in a certain style? If so, why? Try experimenting with different tenses, point of view, etc. Read some of the stories at the end of the book and find out at what point in the writer's career did s/he write the story. At the beginning or late in their career? You will find stylistic changes between the early and later work in any good writer's stories. Try to stay open to developing changes in your own style. This will not only keep you interested in your own work, but challenged by it too.

Many inexperienced writers neglect the fact that style evolves as much from the characters as from their creator. A style that suits your first story may ruin the second, because these characters see the world in different terms from the characters in the first.
    Let's analyze descriptive style through an example:
'Charlie sat on the front door step, cracking one knuckle after

another as he squinted through the curtain of rain which rattled on the tin roofs around him. Waiting for him to come. Dreading the moment when he would see him staggering towards him. Out of focus.'

What have you discovered about Charlie? How did you discover it? Can you see how the writer uses Charlie's body language of 'cracking one knuckle after another' to show how nervous he is? How the bleakness of weather echoes the bleakness of Charlie's life. How the short powerful phrase at the end of the passage 'out of focus' not only refers to the metaphor of 'the curtain of rain' but highlights how 'out of focus' Charlie's life is too.

Contrasting Style and Content

Have you ever read a story in which the style contrasts with the content? Here is an example of what I mean. In Marlene Buono's memorable short story "Offerings" we discover a widow called Emily who goes to her husband's graveside to open a hatbox and lifts out an apology. It's an awkward shape so it takes her an hour to give it the wingspan it needs. Then she places the finished apology on his tombstone and watches it unfold its wings and fly away.

Buono makes a surreal situation accessible through simple description. By coupling the woman's unusual actions with simple prose, the writer has created a story which lingers in the mind. In this story a woman transforms all the apologies she has been given over the years into origami butterflies, birds and pterodactyls.

Whether you want to contrast content and style depends on your intention for the story. E.g. your main character could be a highly successful actor who is florid in speech and actions. You could link this 'florid' man through a florid style of writing. However, what if you want to imply that his inner life is empty? Then you could adopt a sparse style. The reader then has to study the subtext of your story to discover the inner man hidden under a brash exterior.

A writer's style is not immutable; style often changes to suit a given story. Although certain writers have a 'practical' style and others a 'lyrical' style, individual stories by the same writer will often change his or her style, depending on the characters and setting.

Plain prose and simple constructions may reinforce the theme of simplicity. E.g. You want to write a simple story about a rural priest, but a more lyrical style may suggest the complexity of the priest's inner life in contrast to his outer life.

Wait until you have many drafts on paper before you make a final decision on which style you will use. Style should be composed from deliberate decisions made over many drafts of writing as it is an integral part of the story's impact.

N.B. Remember your goal when writing is not to make the writing effortless, but to make it **seem** effortless.

Exercise
1. Transform Charlie into 'Charles', a middle-class boy waiting for his wealthy father. Think about your location, Charles' body language and your descriptive choice of words.

Chapter 14

Walter Mitty's Structure

"The Secret Life of Walter Mitty" by James Thurber appeared in *The New Yorker* on March 18th, 1939.* The structure of the story is interesting as Thurber opens the story [his Point of Entry] immediately with Mitty's fantasy world. The reader believes that the main character in the story is a powerful Naval Commander who is steering his ship through a hurricane. The power of this man is emphasized by the comments of his worshipping crew: 'The old man will get us through' ... 'The Old Man ain't afraid of Hell!'...

It is only when we reach the second paragraph when a woman called Mrs. Mitty shouts ' Not so fast! You're driving too fast.' that we realise, with surprise, that the main character is not a Naval Commander but a meek man called Walter Mitty. We discover that he is merely driving a car in the rain and listening to a deluge of complaints from his nagging wife. It is abundantly obvious that Mitty escapes into his powerful fantasy world to escape the monotony of his life with Mrs. Mitty. The more she nags; the more he escapes. Each fantasy is sparked by an event in his real life. He moves from being a pilot in World War II who saves his crew from a severe storm, to being a world famous surgeon, through to showing immense courage by standing 'tall and proud' in front of a firing squad.

Throughout the story, Thurber contrasts the real life of the character Mitty and his fantasy world as he drives his wife to the

* You can read 'The Secret Life of Walter Mitty' at the end of the book.

hairdressers and then drives around aimlessly as he waits for her. He creates wonderful comedy when Mitty drives past a hospital and imagines himself as a 'surgeon' performing an operation with a fountain pen.

Look how creative Thurber is with his witty use of language: his invention of 'obstreosis of the ductal tract' and 'streptothricosis' and the recurring onomatopoeia of 'ta-pocketa-pocketa-pocketa.' These terms and the absurd, comic medical phrase 'coreopsis has set in' shows us that Thurber not only creates a fantasy world for Mitty but also a fantasy language.

I have met a few Mittyesque characters in my life and I suppose all writers must become like Walter Mitty, to a certain extent, when they write. In fact, it is far better to become Mittyesque than become like a certain man I read about a couple of years ago in a newspaper. Here is his incredible story.

A mild-mannered, elderly man walked into a London Police Station and confessed that he had just strangled his wife of 45 years. The Police didn't believe him. His friends and family didn't believe him, but he insisted that he had indeed strangled her, and as no other suspect was involved, he was charged with murder and the case went to trial. At the court his courtesy and gentleness impressed the judge and jury so much they couldn't believe it either. Surely it was impossible for such a 'nice' man to strangle his beloved wife? It was only when the Judge pressed him further that he explained exactly what had happened.

'Every day was filled with the routine of tea-drinking at certain times, your Honour. Every day I sat opposite my wife and every day my wife stirred her tea thirty times.' He stopped speaking and looked at the judge and jury as if that explained it all. Everyone in the court looked at each other in confusion.

'I don't understand,' the judge murmured. 'How does your

wife's tea-drinking routine have any bearing on her murder?'

'I have had to watch my wife stirring her tea thirty times, ten times a day for forty five years, your Honour. I couldn't stand it any longer.'

'Do you mean to tell me you strangled your wife because she stirred her tea thirty times?' The judge said incredulously.

'Yes,' answered the mild-mannered man quietly.

'Why on earth didn't you just tell her you didn't like it instead of strangling her?' The judge asked the question everyone in the courtroom wanted to ask.

'I didn't like to, your Honour.'

There was an explosion of gasps around the room.

Of course, I've written the scene from my imagination after reading the newspaper article. Imagine – this mild-mannered man was given a life sentence because he was too polite to tell his wife that she irritated him intensely! Isn't that incredible?

After reading this true story, give me a Walter Mitty man every time!

Exercises

1. Create a character whose interior world is more vivid to him/her than the exterior.
2. Decide what genre you're going to write in: comic/ dramatic, etc, then think of ways to contrast both worlds.
3. Write a story in which you 'fool' the reader into thinking that the imaginary world is as real as Thurber does.

[The name Walter Mitty has now entered the English language and has become synonymous with day-dreaming. A 'Mittyesque' character is an ineffectual person who spends more time in fantastic daydreams than in the real world. Or someone who pretends to be someone they're not.]

Chapter 15

Research in Stories

Research used within a story can be fascinating if used subtly, but irritating if it shows.

Look at the following example and you'll see what I mean.

Example 1
"The Pyramids of Ancient Egypt were built as tombs for Kings and Queens, and it was the exclusive privilege to have a Pyramid tomb. However, this tradition only applied in the Old and Middle Kingdoms. Today there are more than 93 Pyramids in Egypt; the most famous ones are those at Giza."

Compare the above with the following extract.

Example 2
"Michael knew that Khufu's pyramid in Giza was built by slaves, but he didn't want to believe it; he didn't want to believe that a man he admired was capable of subjugating an entire race of people. How many slaves had he killed for this pyramid, he wondered? The question was almost as searing as wondering how many lovers his wife had seduced."

In the second extract I hope I have involved you in the life of a man who is looking at the pyramids and trying to make sense of his life; I hope you are interested in what Michael is seeing because you are interested in him. Michael is looking at the past and trying to make sense of his future. Research in short stories should be a back-burner to what your character is experiencing.

Have you heard about the writer who sent her manuscript to an agent but when the agent read it she was stunned to find that the writer had written page after page about the architecture of an old church? I.e. The writer had fallen in love with her research so much that she simply stopped writing the story.

I have been guilty of falling in love with research too, but now I try to weave the research into the fabric of the story by having characters comment on their feelings about what they are seeing/hearing/smelling/touching so that the reader is hardly aware that the research is there.

Use the Internet

We have all heard the maxim write about what you know. I find this very restricting. There is an enormous world out there, but the Internet has brought a lot of it into my study. I can now go on Google Earth and look at roads all over the world; I can place my characters any where in the world if I do enough research and make it sound real. I know this can be done as I wrote a screenplay based in Jamaica in 1830s and every one who has read it has asked me how long I lived there. I've never been. I read many books; both ancient and modern, set in Jamaica in the British Library; looked at photographs and songs, then went on the Internet for more information so that I knew almost as much as if I'd visited the place. If you're interested in research, try to set your story in an unusual setting and see how creative you can be.

Exercises

1. Talk to someone about their work or holiday and use the details in a story.
2. Choose a location and a time in history which informs the plot. [E.g. being in Dallas on a certain day in 1963 and being caught up in the catastrophe.] Place yourself

anywhere in time and make sure you give the readers details from the decade so we are centred in the period. Then place your characters within this setting to create a story full of atmospheric detail.

Chapter 16

Correcting Common Faults

1. Problem. Your story line is confused.
Solution. You have started writing the story without any clear idea of its plot. Read Chapter 2 again and make sure you know exactly what your story is about. I.e. its theme. For example: 'revenge', 'unrequited love', 'redemption', etc. Have you written the outline of your story in bullet points clearly? If not, do so now. Make sure you know exactly whose story you are telling. Is your point of view clear or are you darting around in too many people's heads?

2. Problem. Your story contains too many characters and events.
Solution. Concentrate on which characters and events are vital to the story. Be ruthless and get rid of unnecessary people and events.

3. Problem. You don't care about your main character.
Solution. Try to find some empathetic details about him/her in the past. E.g. if a man is aggressive in the present, show us something that happened to him in the past to make him like this. If you don't care about your main character, why should we?

4. Problem. Your ending is weak or illogical.
Solution. Do you really know your main character well enough? If you know them better than yourself, you should know exactly what they would do at the end of your story.

5. Problem. Your use of language is unoriginal.

Solution. Read Chapter 5 again and think about how to create interesting language using all the tips I've mentioned to 'spice' your writing.

Chapter 17

Revision

Students constantly ask me how I know when my stories/novels are finished. This is one of the most difficult aspects of writing, I believe; knowing when to stop writing only comes from a great deal of experience in writing and revising. It is incredibly easy [and incredibly frustrating] to tinker with a story until you strangle it. In the past, some of my students became so annoyed that their stories weren't 'good enough' that they threw them in the bin. In fact, one of my students [who had been writing for many years before she came to my classes,] threw away years of writing before I could stop her! This is terrible because even if a story isn't well written, there are always small jewels in every story that should be salvaged. If you have written for years and think most of what you've written is worthless, reread everything and lift passages that have merit and put it in a file called 'Ideas'. I have been doing this for years and often discover passages I've written years ago which I've forgotten about, then realise that they are ready to be inserted in stories I've just written.

N. B. Don't waste your words!

The best advice I can give is to 'finish' a story and put it in a drawer for a month. Oh, how can you do that without surreptitious peeks, I can hear you saying? Lock the drawer and give the key to a partner who won't give it back to you! You can't see flaws in a story until you are distanced from it. You might be distanced enough in two weeks but most people need longer. Instead of wanting to reread it, why don't you write another story and immerse yourself in the next plot? All writing, when you are starting out, is an apprenticeship so the more you do, the better you become.

Things To Think About When Revising.

1. Have you started the story late enough? Perhaps half way through some conflict instead of building up to it. Remember you should indicate that the characters had a life before the story starts.
2. Is your plot dramatic enough to carry the story? Is it structured about some conflict? Do you introduce the conflict early enough to hook the reader.
3. Do you know what your key event is? This event should shape the story.
4. Does your story have enough information for the reader to enjoy it or is it too obscure. [There has to be a balance between intriguing hooks and clear explanation.]
5. Is the time sequence in your story clear?
6. Are all your characters really three-dimensional?
7. Are the obstacles you've given your character/s difficult enough?
8. Is your setting appropriate to your plot?
9. Could you cut anything out of your story to make it better?

I can hear you groaning. Have I really got to think about all these problems when I'm writing a short story? Of course not. Just read relevant passages in this book whenever you are having a problem and then carry on writing. If you're not enjoying writing it, it's going to be difficult for a reader to enjoy reading it.

N.B. Writing is a skill like learning to play the piano. You have to practise it a great deal until it [almost] becomes easy.

Chapter 18

Marketing Your Story

Do you know the difference between a person who writes and a writer who perseveres? The writer gets published.

So you've decided you've finished your short story and now you want to submit it. But before you send it out, make certain everything is in order. The quickest way to get a rejection is to send out work that reveals your lack of professionalism. Everything from typing mistakes to wrong format settings or addressing your story to the wrong contact can undermine even the best work. Here are a few things to bear in mind before you send your story out:

Research
1. Is the publication you're submitting your story to the best one for your work? One piece of advice editors always offer to writers is to research the magazine or journal to determine whether or not the piece will fit their needs. Check the submissions guidelines on the web-sites in this chapter.
2. Does the magazine accept your genre of writing? E.g. Science Fiction, Romance, Crime, etc.? Does it accept literary essays or only creative non-fiction?
3. What is the word limit for submissions? Does your work exceed or fit within those limits?
4. How about style? Some magazines like straight-forward, conventional writing; others prefer the experimental or dark. Read past issues of the publication you're submitting your work to and determine whether it fits the editor's needs.

Proof-reading

Once you've narrowed down where you want to submit your work to, ask yourself this question: has my story been thoroughly proof-read? Is it free from typing mistakes and grammatical errors? Proof-reading is always a tricky job, especially when you're proof-reading your own work. Ask other people to proof-read it too. It's often easy to overlook simple errors.

Format

Is the format for your story correct? Does it satisfy the formatting requisites of the publisher or editor? Generally, most publishers and editors prefer a 12 point font in Times New Roman or Arial. A big mistake for any writer is to use different fonts or larger sized fonts to make their story look fancy or elegant. What they do instead is make their work look unprofessional. Before sending out your story, check the editor's submissions guide-lines for the magazine/journal to whom you are submitting your work to make sure what type of format they prefer. If you're sending your story via email, again check with the guide-lines. Some publishers or editors prefer that you cut and paste your work in the body of an e-mail, while others prefer attachments. If the editor prefers attachments, learn what type of file they prefer. There are varying types of files: word documents, rtf files, text edit. Make certain that you submit your work in a format that is readable for said publisher or editor.

Cover Letter

Always include a cover letter with your submission.

Is the address listed in the cover letter correct? Did you address the letter to the correct person? Most editors of magazines aren't in charge of reading submissions. Some magazines will even have departments for fiction, poetry, non-fiction, etc. Make certain you're sending the letter to the right department and person before submitting.

If you have some writing credits, then list where your work has been published before. If not, it's best not to state anything at all on the subject. Some publishing houses or literary magazines are always on the look out for new or emerging writers. If your work is good enough and fits their needs, it will get noticed. Above all, make your covering letter concise and interesting.

Records

Once you've followed these guidelines and submitted your work, keep a record of when and to whom you submitted your story and if it was accepted or rejected. From your records, you'll be able to know how long your story was in circulation and whether or not you should contact the publication. It's important to keep records or you might find yourself sending the same story to the same editor six months later as one of my students did!

Also, pay close attention to whether or not the publication you're submitting your work to has specific reading periods. Some magazines, especially University Literary Magazines, will only read stories during certain times of the year. Don't make the mistake of submitting your work when the publication isn't reading submissions.

Courtesy

As with any business, being courteous goes a long way in building a strong reputation with publishers or editors. Once you've submitted your work, there will inevitably be a waiting time before you hear from an editor or publisher. Sometimes this can be as short as two weeks, [especially if you're submitting electronically] or as long as six to twelve months. Magazines, particularly literary magazines, are often cash-strapped and can't afford a lot of readers to read stories. That means the slush pile can back up for months before your work ever reaches the hands of the first reader. So sending out stories requires a great deal of patience. If more than three months has passed, you should send out a brief letter or email to inquire about the status of your story.

Another rule of law regarding submissions is whether or not the publication accepts simultaneous submissions. Again, determine what their policy on this issue is in the submissions guidelines. Some publications absolutely forbid it, while others will accept it. It depends on the magazine or publisher. Some magazines have very rigid publishing schedules and would like to know that the rights to the story they've accepted is available. If the publication has First Rights or Exclusive Rights, then simultaneous submissions will most likely be off the table. Other magazines are lax about this policy. Most editors understand the time and commitment that writers put into their work and try to make allowances.

Professionalism is a necessary component to becoming a published writer. Writing, like anything else, is a profession and editors and publishers will only want to work with writers who know their business as well as their craft. By following these guidelines, you'll be able to project a professional attitude when you submit your work and maximize your chances of seeing your name in print.

Rejection

The one thing that all writers have to overcome is fear of rejection. However, it is good to remember that the editor is not rejecting you, but one piece of writing. Learn to overcome rejection by a simple strategy – always send more than one story out at a time, so if one is returned, you always have another in the pipe-line. Then immediately send out another and finish writing a third, so you always live in hope. It's a technique that I've used for years and it works! However, you can minimize the number of rejections you receive by studying Chapter 13's Top Tips and polishing your story until it shines.

Before you send your story to anyone, do this important exercise: imagine that a friend, who's in a hurry, asks you 'what's your story about?' You have to hook him in a couple of minutes. If you can't interest people, there's either a problem with the focus of your story or your 'pitching' I.e. the way you're 'selling' your story. If lack of focus is the problem, reread this book and rewrite. If pitching is your problem, write out numerous very brief synopses of your story and try them out on friends and family. You'll know which version is best because it will engage them immediately. E.g. 'Jon is an angry seventeen-year-old who was abandoned in a children's home for ten years and doesn't know why. He decides to hunt for his family to seek revenge, but discovers his grandfather who transforms his life in a totally unexpected way.' Are you hooked? Do you want to know why Jon was abandoned? Do you want to know how his grandfather transformed his life? If you can make people ask you more questions about your story, you're ready to send it out to an editor.

I've mentioned how Ernest Hemingway could hook the reader in a few words: "For sale: baby shoes, never worn."

Look at how two other writers do it.
"Longed for him. Got him. Shit." Margaret Atwood
[Humorous brevity]

"The baby's blood type? Human, mostly." Orson Scott Card
[Intriguing brevity]

Practise writing a brief premise of your own stories in the same way and use them in a covering letter to 'hook' editors. Writing this concisely is wonderfully productive in teaching you how to use words effectively.

SUMMARY

1. Send out a brief, well-written letter to a submissions editor, which includes the great pitch you've written, [Look at the blurbs on the back of good books to give you an idea of intriguing brevity.] Write a couple of interesting lines about yourself.

Look at the difference between:

A. 'I'm a 50 year housewife who's hoping you're going to accept this story as I haven't published anything before.' Or worse 'This is my best story so I'm sure you'll publish it.'

B. 'I'm great at multi-tasking and each day I survive loud garage music, three challenging teenage sons, cleaning, cooking, nursing, acting as chauffeur and writing on the kitchen table with a Labrador chewing my Emilio Pucci shoes.'

Which version would interest you on a cold, wet Monday morning? Note the shoes. A small, intriguing detail. How is the editor to know that you write in old slippers? Try to find something in your own life which will interest or entertain editors. Put them in a good mood, ready to read your story.

2. Do remember to send an editor EXACTLY what they want. Don't send them romantic stories if they want wry humorous ones and vice versa.

3. If they want a double-spaced story in size 12 font – give them exactly that.

4. Most editors are swamped with stories, so make your package stand out from the crowd by your profession-

alism. Use good quality paper, double-spacing and a story that is left justified only.

3. Don't send a long story, if a journal or magazine is looking for stories under 2,000 words.

4. Always ensure that you've addressed your letter to the right person. Nobody likes receiving a letter with someone else's name on it. So how can you make sure you do this? Pluck up your courage and ring up a magazine to ask if 'so and so' is still the right person to send your story to. If s/he has moved on, write down the new name. Ask if 'so and so' would be interested in – here you pitch your story – very briefly. [Look how Hemingway did it!] Perhaps the person will ask you some questions about your story and already you've got a dialogue going. Thank her for her time. You'll be amazed at how much more receptive people are if you are interested in them and remember their names. And you've practiced your pitch too! Great.

Aldous Huxley once wrote 'it is not how we cope with success that makes us strong, but how we cope with failure.' Look at how many times famous writers' words have been rejected in the past. It is only through their perseverance that they became published. You can too.

Chapter 19

Top tips For Short Story Writing

- Start the story with an intriguing/shocking/funny/thought-provoking or poignant opening sentence.
- Characterisation. Create an engaging and sympathetic lead character with whom the reader can identify, and from whose point of view the story is told.
- The Plot. Confront this lead character with a vital and urgent conflict [problem] which s/he must, but seemingly cannot, solve.
- Raising the tension. Increase the problems which the main character faces. I.e. Each attempt the character makes to resolve his/her problems actually increases them.
- Bring the story to its climax point, where the main character faces apparent defeat. This is both the emotional and dramatic height of the action. At this point, s/he must choose a course of action — whether it's right or wrong.
- Develop a solution or resolution of the conflict in which the lead character finally resolves her conflict, restoring some tranquillity to her life . . . or . . . perhaps she fails to overcome the problem [to get what she wants], but nevertheless gains some deeper insight into life through her defeat.
- Setting the scene. Locate this character in a place which is full of romantic/ mysterious/ magical or fantastical atmosphere. [Depending on the type of story you wish to tell.]
- Think about the imagery you want to create. Is your language full of fresh metaphors and similes or stale ones? Is your character using all of his/her senses or are you merely using sight?
- Are you writing your character's dialogue from your POV

or from theirs? Forget yourself and delve deep into your character's past life and learn to see through her/his eyes. Then the dialogue will flow from them, not you.

- Keep adverbs; I.e. 'slowly', 'happily', 'quietly' to a minimum as they weaken sentences.
- Make your verbs work hard. E.g. 'She crept across the room' tells us about a character's state of mind – 'walked' tells us nothing.
- Use the active, rather than the passive voice in sentences – it's stronger. Think of a comic rephrasing of an old joke and you'll know what I mean: why was the road crossed by the chicken?
- Is the title of your story intriguing?
- Don't send out any material until you have proof-read it thoroughly to erase all mistakes.
- Make sure you send your material to an editor/publisher who is looking for your type of story. I.e. know your markets.

Chapter 20

UK Writing Outlets

Most U.K. magazines still prefer to receive submissions by post rather than email. Email submissions clog up in-boxes and need to be printed off for editors, who would still rather read hard copies.

Print the story on one side of the paper only and use a size 12 font for easy reading. Many magazines ask for a S.A.E so that they can return your story if rejected, but this can be expensive and useless to writers as a crumpled story can't be used again. A cheaper [and more psychologically satisfying strategy] is to send a S.A.E using a DL sized envelope – too small for your story to be returned, but large enough for a letter from the magazine.

Do remember to include your name and contact number on every page of a short story. [Unless an outlet doesn't want it.] I always put my contact details in the footer, using a size 8 font so it does not intrude on the reader's concentration on the story.]

Always read the magazine you are submitting to before sending off your story. Get a feel for the readership and the style of stories accepted. This is very important. Don't waste everyone's time by sending in the type of story that a magazine never publishes. It just annoys an editor and makes you poorer and depressed.

Send seasonal stories well in advance. Most magazines work six months in advance and stories for seasonal issues are selected well in advance of publication.

Payment varies from magazine to magazine. Guidelines will be given on websites or by the editorial department of the magazines. Some magazines are non-profit making so will only offer a writer token payment, but getting published in a good magazine can help your writing career enormously as you will find other magazines and journals will become more interested in publishing your work if you have a publishing record.

There is a wealth of writing outlets out there. Here are only some that I've discovered which will help you to market your work. Do check out these outlets - they can help you achieve writing success.

Albedo One
http://www.albedo1.com
Ireland's foremost magazine of the fantastic are always looking for thoughtful, well written fiction. Their definition of what constitutes science fiction, horror and fantasy is extremely broad. They love to see material which pushes at the boundaries.

Their preferred length is between 2,500 and 8,000 words. Their response time is variable - mostly between two and four months.

They only accept previously unpublished stories, and do not accept simultaneous submissions.

All submissions should be typewritten, on A4 paper or US equivalent, double-spaced, using one side of the paper and leaving at least 1" margins all round. Softcopy should be available on request.

Their address:
Albedo One
2 Post Road
Lusk
Co. Dublin
Ireland.

They also need ezine stories and will accept E-submissions, but no attachments.

Payment is €3 per 1,000 words (Euro)

Submission Guidelines:

http://www.albedo1.com/html/writers_guidelines.html

Ambit Magazine

http://www.ambitmagazine.co.uk

Ambit contains unsolicited, previously unpublished poetry and short fiction submissions. Their style tends towards the shocking, the erotic, the comic and the provocative. This magazine is well regarded in the UK and is non-profit making.

If you decide your work is right for them, send two or three stories up to 10,000 words in length to: Ambit, 17 Priory Gardens, London N6 5QY, UK.

N.B. Don't send work via email as they won't read it.

Black Static

http://www.ttapress.com

Wants submissions of new horror short stories up to 8,000 words.

It is strongly recommended that you study the magazine before submitting as this will obviously greatly improve your chances of acceptance.

They publish modern dark fantasy and horror, as well as borderline material which uses genre elements with a relatively mainstream sensibility.

At the time of print, the magazine pays £30/1000 words on publication (3p UK per word).

Submission Guidelines:

http://www.ttapress.com/blackstatic/guidelines/

Dream Catcher Magazine

Dream Catcher is an international journal, a small press and a community-based literature organisation, located in the East Midlands. [Although the editor of Dream Catcher is Canadian.]

It welcomes a vast range of submissions from well known and unknown writers. It is interested in quality and diversity. The journal welcomes poetry, short-stories, artwork, interviews and reviews. Most short-stories are about 2000 words, but there are exceptions. If it's long and good it will be published.

In Issue 23 they published a remarkable range of writings from Canada. How many of us really know Canadian poets and short story writers? Most of us know of Margaret Atwood and Alice Munro, but what about other names? Each issue of this journal introduces us to more and more writers. [You could be one of them!]

It only accepts email submissions from overseas authors, who should send their work to info@dreamcatchermagazine.co.uk

UK authors should send their work to:

The Editor

Dream Catcher Magazine

4 Church Street

Market Rasen

Lincoln LN8 3ET

Log onto http://www.dreamcatchermagazine.co.uk for more details.

This magazine will inspire you as readers and stimulate you as writers, so why not subscribe to it?

East of the Web

East of the Web is keen to provide exposure for writers by offering them a place where their work will be seen and read on a respected site. The site receives about half a million unique page views per month, so successful submissions are likely to be viewed by more readers than in almost any other short story publication. In addition, the site receives attention from agents, the press, film makers, schools, universities and other publishers.

Obviously this is a site that is well worth visiting and submitting stories to. Read some of the stories before you submit to them to get a flavour of the type of story they like.

An encouraging tale: one of my students posted a short story on this site. It was read by an agent who asked her if she would rewrite it as a novel. She did and gained not only an agent, but a large advance for her book which was published in 2006!

Website: http://www.eastoftheweb.com/short-stories

Fractured West

Fractured West is a print magazine for flash fiction. They want readers to see things in a different way so they are looking for writers who write things in a different way. They want to be surprised, so surprise them!

They are particularly interested in new, unpublished, and emerging writers.

Send your best work in the body of an email to submissions@fracturedwest.com

They want stories under 500 words and only one story at a time.

More information at

http://www.fracturedwest.com/submissions

Granta Magazine

Granta Magazine has a belief in the power and urgency of the story, both in fiction and non-fiction, and the story's supreme ability to describe, illuminate and make real. The Observer wrote of *Granta*: 'In its blend of memoirs and photojournalism, and in its championing of contemporary realist fiction, Granta has its face pressed firmly against the window, determined to witness the world.'

They focus mainly on fiction, memoir, and reportage, with a bias towards the interesting and unusual. They only publish original material. I.e. first-ever publication - so they will not publish a story that has already appeared on the web or elsewhere in print.

They state that they have no set minimum or maximum length for submissions, but most of their submissions are between 3,000-6,000 words.

Please do not send more than story at one time. Submissions should be made by post only as emails are not accepted.

They aim to respond to submissions within a month of receipt.

The address for submissions is:

The Editor

Granta Magazine,A

12 Addison Avenue,A

London W11 4QR

The Horizon Review

This Review is an online review of literature and art. It publishes poems, stories, essays, articles and memoir and multimedia pieces. It appears twice a year in March and September.

They only accept email submissions at submissions-horizon@saltpublishing.com and ask that you put your submission into one document, either .doc or .rtf.

Send a maximum of three short stories and a 75 word biographical note. You need to read their submission guidelines carefully as they are specific.

Website:

http://www.saltpublishing.com/horizon/submissions

Irish Pages

This is a biannual journal, edited in Belfast that publishes writing from Ireland and overseas.

They only accept postal submissions, but phone or email queries regarding the submission process are accepted. Tel: 0044

(0) 28 90434800

Email: editor@irishpages.org

Submissions, in both Irish or English, should be sent to the editor at the following address:

Irish Pages

The Linen Hall Library

17 Donegall Square North

Belfast BT1 5GB

Website: http://www.irishpages.org

Liars' League

This is a monthly collaborative event held in London for writers and actors. Each month new stories are chosen and read by an actor. If you want to submit a story, here's what the organizers are looking for:

Entertaining stories between 800 – 2,000 long submitted to liarsleague@yahoo.co.uk

Obviously choose a story that can be enjoyed through a live performance, not one which needs several readings to be understood.

They meet on the second Tuesday of every month at a pub in Central London. [Five minutes away from Oxford Tube Station.]

The Phoenix

37 Cavendish Square

London

W1G 0PP

Check out their interesting website to find out more information about the organizers and the actors they use.

http://liarsleague.typepad.com

Mslexia Magazine

For women writers. It has a clear target audience and remit which marks it out from the other writers' magazines and contains a lot of very useful articles.

There are 15 pages of new writing in each issue; a creativity section and also useful listings of workshops and writing events, etc.

For women writers who are aiming at the more literary end of the spectrum, *Mslexia* is very good. A lot more information can be found at their web-site:

Website: http://www.mslexia.co.uk

New Welsh Review

New Welsh Review brings you some vibrant and engaging writing from Wales. The magazine contains articles on literature, theatre and the arts, as well as interviews, reviews, new fiction and poetry, plus a photo essay, opinion column and an exploration of the writer's craft. It aims to reflect and stimulate the literary scene now, celebrating both contemporary writing and the literary tradition.

Submission of short stories should be made by post or email.

Postal submissions - should be sent to the editor accompanied by a covering letter and a stamped addressed envelope or international money order for return. To this address:

New Welsh Review
PO Box 170
Aberystwyth,
Ceredigion
SY23 1WZ S. Wales.

Email submissions of one short story in any three-month period should be sent to submissions@newwelshreview.com. Please title your email 'Submissions' and attach your work as a word document. They ask that you also include a covering letter.

Short stories must be typed, single-sided and double-spaced, in the region of 2,500 to 3,000 words.

They pay in the region of £80 for a short story upon publication.

Park Publications

They currently publish three quarterly magazines: *Scribble*; their short fiction magazine, has been around since early 1999 and contains quality short stories from new and established writers. In December 2007, *Scribble* was awarded the title 'Best UK Short Fiction Magazine' in the Writers' Grand Circle Awards. *Countryside Tales* was launched in 2000 and contains poetry, articles and short stories with a countryside feel.

Newer writers may be interested in their newest fiction magazine, and critique service. The magazine, titled *'Debut'*, is aimed primarily (but not exclusively) at unpublished writers and offers the chance to have work assessed by an experienced fiction editor.

They publish fiction, poetry, anthologies and run writing competitions.

Short Stories of any genre up to 3,000 words are accepted.

Postal address:

14 The Park,

Stow On The Wold

Cheltenham

Glos.

GL54 1DX

TEL: 01451 831053

E-mail : enquiries@parkpublications.co.uk

For more information log onto:

http://www.parkpublications.co.uk

QWF [Quality Women's Fiction] Magazine

This bi-monthly perfect bound magazine in A5 format publishes around 12 short stories by women in every issue and pays £10 for each one.

QWF will not consider stories of the type found in the women's weekly magazines.

The editors want stories about women's lives: motherhood,

marriage and partnerships, dealing with aging parents, maybe, or bereavement.

The maximum word count for stories is usually 4,000 words, but the editors will consider stories which exceed that if they have great potential, but very rarely publish anything over 5,000 words. They also need stories which come in at around 1,600 words as these are useful 'fillers'.

The editors are big fans of Helen Dunmore, Alice Munro, Kate Atkinson, Lorrie Moore, Helen Simpson, Elizabeth Bowen and Elizabeth Jane Howard, and advise would-be contributors to *QWF* to read some of their short stories before submitting.

'At *QWF* we want to encourage female short story writers, and always take time to give feedback on those stories we reject,' says Jo Good. 'If writers don't want this kind of feedback, then please can they say so in their covering letter.'

It's very useful to have expert feed-back on any story you submit, so why not try this magazine?

All stories for possible inclusion in QWF should be sent to:

Sally Zigmond, 18 Warwick Crescent, Harrogate, N Yorks HG2 8JA. email: szigmond@another.com.

Scarlet

Advertised as: The Magazine that Turns Women On.

9 Richett Street. Fulham. London. SW6 1RU

Publishes Fiction and Erotica. Contact Deputy Editor for fiction.

N.B. *Scarlett* is aimed at women between 20 – 40.

Email: sarah@helixmedia.co.uk

Website: www.scarletmagazine.co.uk

Scheherazade

14 Queen's Park Rise. Brighton. BN2 9ZF

A literary magazine that publishes Fantasy, Science Fiction and Gothic Romance short stories. Accepts email queries. Look at the website for more information.

Email: editor@schez.co.uk

Website: www.schez.co.uk

Stand Magazine

It is a respected quarterly literary magazine run by Leeds University.

Submission Guidelines

Stand can only consider previously unpublished material.. Manuscripts should be accompanied by a SASE or, in the case of manuscript sent from abroad to the editors at the address in Leeds, by sufficient International Reply Coupons (IRC) to cover return postage. (Note: These are often only available at larger post offices in the USA.) Fiction submissions under 3,000 words are preferred.

Manuscripts should be sent to:

The Editors

Stand Magazine

School of English

Leeds University

Leeds LS2 9JT

England

North American submissions should be sent to:

David Latané

Stand Magazine

Department of English

Virginia Commonwealth University Richmond,

VA 23284-2005

USA

Website:

http://www.people.vcu.edu/~dlatane/stand-maga/submis-sions.html

Shortbread

Shortbread is an online community of short story readers and writers. It's free to join. Joining gives you the ability to read, listen and download stories online, participate in the community and if you're an author, showcase your work and enter short story writing competitions. They also regularly select the best stories to produce in professional audio format.

Website: http://www.shortbreadstories.co.uk

The Edge

They state on their website that this is the 'Sharpest Magazine In The World.' After a comment like that you have to look at their stories to see if you agree. However, they have published an impressive list of writers whose names you will see on their website. If you think that your writing is 'sharp enough', then this is the outlet for you. More details on:

http://www.theedge.abelgratis.co.uk

The London Magazine

They accept ideas for art reviews, memoir pieces, fiction, poetry and poetry reviews. They prefer e-mail, with the poems or stories to be sent in the body of the email, as well as in attachment.

Please send your submissions to admin@thelondon-magazine.net. All postal submissions must be accompanied by a stamped and addressed envelope.

Please send all postal submissions and/or enquiries to: The London Magazine, Flat 5, 11 Queen's Gate, London, SW7 5EL.

Unfortunately, at the moment, because of the cancellation of their Arts Council Grant, the magazine is unable to pay its writers. However, it is a well regarded publication. As it states on their website 'The London Magazine is a meeting place of the day's greatest minds.'

Website: http://thelondonmagazine.co.uk

The One Million Stories Creative Writing Project
This is a friendly creative space run by and for writers. They want to attract and showcase the best writing in the English Language from across the globe.

In their words: 'The writers we publish want to re-write the world in their own imagination, and attempt to make sense of the strange times in which we live. We hope the stories published on our site capture what you are thinking and feeling.' They would like some feedback from readers of the site and also your short stories between 50-5000 words.

They are giving writers a challenge called the 52 Shorts Challenge to encourage writers to write a short story every week of the year. Wow! Even if you can't fulfil this challenge, you might be stimulated to write a story on a theme they give you each week.

Log onto http://www.millionstories.net

The New Writer
This magazine is aimed at all writers who write short stories, novels and articles; in short, anyone who seriously wants to be published. It was launched in September 1996 and every issue contains original short stories, poetry, articles, book reviews, market information, news and readers' views.

If you are starting out as a writer, I'd recommend that you subscribe to this very useful magazine, especially as they will only commission short stories from subscribers and prizewinners of their competitions. Each issue contains up to four short stories from subscribers and guest writers, limited to a maximum 4,000 words on any theme and in any genre. No multiple submissions. Providing SAE accompanies each script, a tick-sheet is enclosed with the returned story to provide feedback and advice where applicable. Payment: £10 per story payable by credit voucher on publication.

Address

PO Box 60 Cranbrook Kent TV17 2ZR
Contact phone: 01580 212626

It is published six times a year.
Website: http://www.thenewwriter.com

The Review

4, Algar House, Webber Row, London. SE1 8QT.
Telephone: 0207 261 1134
Publishes contemporary short fiction and poetry.
[Used to be based in America and Canada, but now moved to London.]
Email: editor@thereview.freeserve.co.uk

The Stinging Fly

This magazine is based in Ireland. Its main objective is to bring out a well-designed publication that provides a forum for the very best new Irish and international writing. They believe that there is a need for a magazine that gives new and emerging writers an opportunity to get their work out into the world. They are particularly concerned to provide an outlet for short story writers. Each issue features several short stories and sometimes they also devote entire issues to new fiction when they feel like it!

It is a non-profit making concern so there is only a token payment, but it is well worth sending in a short story as the magazine is beautifully presented, imaginatively designed and full of interesting material.

All work submitted must be previously unpublished and ideally should not be under consideration elsewhere.

They do not accept e-mail submissions, so post your story to:
The Stinging Fly,
PO Box 6016,
Dublin 8,

Ireland.

More information at

http://www.stingingfly.org/submissions.html

The Weekly News

2 Albert Square, Dundee, Tayside. DD1 9QJ

Telephone: 01382 22131

Accepts queries by email. Accepts stories of up to 1,200. Sample copy and manuscript guidelines are free on request. A media pack is available online.

Email: dburness@dcthomson.co.uk

Website: www.dcthomson.co.uk

N.B. Check their submissions section very carefully before sending them any material.

Woman's Weekly

Woman's Weekly Fiction publishes short stories between 1000 and 6000 words each, on subjects ranging from humour, romance to crime. The stories should appeal to older women.

Log onto their website to see if your writing style suits them.

Address:

IPC Media Ltd King's Reach Tower

Stamford Street

London SE1 9LS.

It's never too early to send in seasonal stories.

Contact the Fiction Editor for more details.

Website: www.ipcmedia.com

Writing Magazine

Writers' News and *Writing Magazine* have competition programmes, with lots of prizes and extra opportunities for short story and poetry winners to be published, either in print or online.

All first prize-winning short stories will be published in

Writers' News or *Writing Magazine* as appropriate; second and third prize-winning stories will be published on their website. 5th Floor, 31-32 Park Row, Leeds, LS1 5JD.

Telephone: 01133 2002929

This magazine publishes Adventure, Historical Romance, Horror, Science Fiction, Confession, Humorous, Erotica, Mainstream, Ethnic, Mystery, Suspense, Experimental, Western, Fantasy and Religious Short Stories. See their web-site for more details:

www.writersnews.co.uk

Writer's Forum

This magazine was established in 1995. It publishes articles on writing techniques and runs monthly poetry and short story competitions. The editor welcomes short stories, articles and reviews. Contributor's guidelines are available on their website.

Competitions in *Writers' Forum* have a rolling deadline unless otherwise stated. A story or poem that misses the cut-off point for one issue will simply be included in the next contest.

All entries must be original and previously unpublished – this includes newspapers, magazines, books and websites.

Publication on private online forums that are password-protected and in private letters and emails does not count. By entering, entrants agree for their stories and poems to be published in *Writers' Forum* if successful. They have no current plans to produce anthologies but reserve the right to include any winning entries in any such projects in the future. Copyright remains with the author.

The competitions are open to all nationalities worldwide, but entries must be in English.

More information on their website:

http://www.writers-forum.com

X Magazine

www.flippedeye.net/xmag

PO Box 43771, London W14 8zy

Telephone: 0845 430 9517

Accepts completed manuscripts of no more than 5,000 words. Contemporary and experimental short fiction. Prefers material from writing groups in order to focus on a few writers from a group.

You Write On

http://www.youwriteon.com

The aim of YouWriteOn.com is to help all writers to get noticed and published.

To get started, you must join www.YouWriteOn.com which is free.

Then upload your opening chapters or short stories – novel chapters must be fiction opening chapters between 6,000 to 10,000 words, and fiction short stories between 2,000 to 5,000 words, to qualify for the 'YouWriteOn' Top Ten and a professional critique.

Once uploaded, your chapters or stories will be automatically sent out for review to another member.

Each month the top five writers on the web-site's 'Top Ten' receive a free professional critique from established authors and editors from leading literary agents and publishers, including Curtis Brown, Orion and Bloomsbury.

The top five chapters/stories each month enter their Best Sellers Chart. This Chart is a showcase for the highest rated stories on the site. See the web-site for further details of the chart rules and how stories enter the Top Ten and Best Seller charts.

Literary professionals decide on the winners for the site's Book of The Year Award from all the stories that enter their Best Sellers Chart.

SMALL PRESSES

Cinnamon Press

This is a small, independent publisher run by a family team and based in North Wales.

Cinnamon is an innovative publisher, publishing fiction, poetry and selective non fiction books. They are looking for work that is thought-provoking and has something new to say.

Their list includes books from Wales, Scotland and England and also titles from Ireland, South Africa, New Zealand, America and China.

Bi-annually, it also runs competitions for writers of poetry, novels/novellas and short stories.

Log onto http://www.cinnamonpress.com/competitions for more details.

Their bi-annual competitions are an excellent way of competing for publication in novel/novella, poetry and short story genres.

They are currently closed for submissions outside their competitions, but they state that they are constantly reviewing their submissions policy so it is well worth logging onto

http://www.cinnamonpress.com/submissions to check on the latest news.

Comma Press

Comma Press is a not-for-profit publishing initiative dedicated to promoting new fiction and poetry, with an emphasis on the short story. It is committed to a spirit of risk-taking and challenging publishing, free of the commercial pressures on mainstream houses.

Here is what they say on their website: 'Something happens in good short stories which is quite unique to them as a form; the imaginary worlds they create are coloured slightly differently to those of the novel. Their protagonists are more independent and intriguing. The realities they depict more arbitrary, accidental and amoral. *Comma* believes British publishing is missing out on something in its neglect of the short story and to make up for it we are currently the most prolific hardcopy publisher of short stories in the country.'

How wonderful to find a publisher promoting the genre of the short story. And how gratifying it must be that the 2010 winner of the prodigious BBC National Short Story Award is one of their authors; poet and short story writer, David Constantine, for his story *"Tea At The Midland"*. Here is what James Naughtie, Chair of the Judges, wrote about the story: ...'It is remarkable for the rich poetry at its heart and the economy with which David Constantine creates a story with fully formed characters and a memorable setting. It has imagination, depth and brevity.'

Indeed, everything that a good short story should contain.

Comma accepts one or two stories for their bi-annual 'new writer' showcase; all other projects are by commission only.

Check out their interesting website: http://www.comma-press.co.uk

Flambard Press

Flambard is an independent press publishing poetry and fiction. It has a history of nurturing new and neglected writers from Britain and beyond. Their contemporary list continues to grow in innovative and challenging directions. Although *Flambard* now publishes a diverse collection of books from all over the world, they remain especially supportive of writers from northern England.

They consider only book-length collections of poetry or short stories, and novels. For short story writers who wish to submit, please send 3 or 4 stories and a contents page; for novelists, a synopsis and the opening chapters.

They accept both postal and email submissions.

Postal submissions to:

Holy Jesus Hospital
City Road
Newcastle upon Tyne
NE1 2AS
UK
Tel: (0191) 233 3865
Fax: (01434) 674178
And email submissions to submit@flambardpress.co.uk.

Send a Word file with the title of your novel or collection in the subject line.

RADIO 4

Did you know that five days a week, fifty-two weeks a year, each afternoon at 3.30, the BBC broadcasts a short story on Radio 4? There are also stories to be heard on weekend evenings and some are dramatized for play slots such as the Afternoon Play. For some years, the BBC has been the biggest single commissioner and champion of the short story in the UK.

Their output ranges from the best classic and recently published works, to newly commissioned stories on a vast range of subjects and from all points of the globe. If you listen to short stories on BBC Radio, [and I hope you do] you'll find that they usually come in clusters of five, either by a single author [often taken from a recent collection] or linked by a theme, which is used as a springboard for commissioning work by five different writers.

Different producers, both in-house and independent, have directed stories from new collections by Lesley Hart, Matthew Kneale, Mary Yukari Waters and Mick Jackson; there have also been a number of classic collections from past masters of the art like Elizabeth Taylor, Margaret Bonham and Oscar Wilde.

Beyond these however, the BBC has been responsible for commissioning around 40 weeks of stories written directly for broadcast. There have been stories drawn from the Borderlands by writers such as Stevie Davies, Alison Fell and the late Julia Darling; tales of Wild Ways from Bosnia to the American Highway - by writers such as Kate Pullinger, Emily Perkins and Louise Doughty; and stories set on board overnight trains from Shanghai to Beijing, Vienna to Bucharest, Glasgow to Euston. Other tales firmly rooted in location came from Cornwall, the Bath Festival and Brighton.

"Theories of Relativity" celebrated the hundredth anniversary of Einstein's discovery with stories about Einstein in an alternative life as a locksmith and as a time-traveller sharing philosophies and ginger nuts with a car park attendant! A second series of "Curly Tales" played with the story-telling form and turned it upside down.

Most of the stories are single-voice readings recorded in a studio, often read by some of the greatest names in British theatre, occasionally by the author, but always produced with great sympathy for each voice. Sometimes locations take a role: in "Poor, Obscure, Plain and Little", five writers were asked to write a story inspired by Jane Eyre, which were then recorded in Howarth.

Sometimes fiction is mixed with fact; in a series "From The Pennines", stories were mixed with actual recordings from the area. Recordings are also made at literary festivals, and in front of audiences. Occasionally stories are told using two voices, or music or effects.

The story slots on Radio 4 run to fourteen minutes, which means stories are either written to a specific length - approximately 2000 words - or abridged if already published. The fees for writers are small but the exposure is large - the current audience figures for the afternoon slot are 1.3 million listeners a week. And agents listen to the radio too!

Radio 4 states that you can break all the rules of story-telling if the writing or the characters are strong enough. [However, don't break the rules of story-telling until you know what they are!]

However, for radio, it is worth remembering that the audience cannot look back to the beginning, so the plot needs to be clear and the characters not too numerous. Jumps in time and place can be hard to negotiate for even the most skilled reader; remember too that unbroken, though beautifully lyrical prose can wash over the audience, who will probably be busy doing other things at the same time.

Dialogue is often the ideal way to break up long passages and re-capture the audience's attention. Finally, bear in mind that Radio 4 stories are on air in the middle of the afternoon, when children may be listening and that the BBC will not broadcast anything offensive or unsuitable in content or language for a daytime audience.

Recorded Radio Stories

http://www.shortstoryradio.com.

A site well worth submitting a story to as they will be recorded by a professional actor and published on this website. The recorded story will be available to hear for twelve months from the date of the first transmission. The writers of chosen stories will also receive a profile in the 'Our Writers' section of the website.

Here are some of their guide lines:

'Writers of any nationality are welcome to submit a story, but the story must be written in English. There is no restriction on period or style but the story must be fictional. Maximum 3,000 words. Stories should not contain expletives or content of an overtly sexual or violent nature.'

Stories submitted for consideration must not have been published or broadcast previously [including but not limited to print, online or audio formats] and must be original pieces of work written by the writer who has submitted the story.

You will receive email confirmation once your story has been received, but only writers whose stories are accepted for broadcast will be notified. No further correspondence will be entered into once work has been submitted. If you do not hear from them within 4 weeks of submitting your story please assume that on this occasion they have chosen not to accept your story

Writers may submit only one short story at a time, but are free to submit up to ten short stories in any six month period.'

Short Story Net

Do you want to read short stories on line? Do you want readers to read and comment on your story on line? If you do, then this is a site worth looking at.

They have many different genres to choose from such as flash fiction, romance and humour, etc. These short stories are written by authors from all over the world.

http://www.short-story.net

Short Story Library.

This is a free weekly online magazine which accepts poetry, micro-fiction, flash fiction and short stories and publishes them on the web. They accept submissions all year round and try to respond within six weeks.

The magazine was formed in May 2008 and has enjoyed a constant growth ever since. If you enjoy the magazine, the editors ask that you sign up for the free weekly newsletter to be notified when their new issues are released.

Have a look at the following website and see if you'd be interested in submitting to this site. They are looking for short stories up to 5,000 words.

Website: http://shortstory.us.com

UK Authors' International Writers' Website

Yet another useful site which will give you even more outlets for your work in small presses and magazines! It also has lists of

publishers, agents, [in UK and USA] a number of Writers' Resources, Writers Circles and more. [Double-check the outlets as some could be out-of-date. E.g. "The Lights List of Small Presses" is no longer being published.]
Website: http://genres.ukauthors.com

The Short Story Site
And if I haven't given you enough UK sites, here's one which will give you hundreds more! Incredibly useful!
http://www.theshortstory.org.uk/magazines

American Outlets

The American short story market is far bigger than that of the UK. You will discover numerous outlets on http://duotrope.com

This is an invaluable site for writers all over the world. It is an award-winning free writers' resource listing over 3200 current Fiction and Poetry publications! Use this site to search for markets that may be ideal for the story you've just polished. There are also menus at the top and right of each page that offers more free services to writers and editors. Duotrope states that it make several updates per day and check each of the current listings around once a week to ensure the site is the most up-to-date database humanly possible.

Duotrope is the most amazing marketing resource I've seen; it is well worth checking its outlets regularly.

Here are some of the sites listed on *Duotrope* and also many others I have discovered.

A Gathering of the Tribes

A Gathering of the Tribes is an arts and cultural organization dedicated to excellence in the arts from a diverse perspective. It has been in existence since 1991 and is located on the Lower East Side of New York City.

It accepts short stories of up to 3,500 words, but you have a better chance with shorter work. Your name should appear on each page. You may send a cover letter with a short bio, contact return address info. Submissions may be stapled or paper-clipped together with cover info. They are looking for many different styles: literary, political satire, magical realism, lyrical narratives, contemporary fiction, historical fiction with an emphasis on multiculturalism and alternative viewpoints.

More information on http://www.tribes.org/web

Aberrant Dreams

http://www.hd-image.com/aberrant_dreams/index.htm
Aberrant Dreams accepts short fiction of any genre, though they primarily focus on the genres of fantasy, science fiction, and supernatural horror. They want stories with a solid plot and good character development. Stories should be original and not a rehash of tired old themes. If you do use an old theme, add a twist to make it unique. Submit to the appropriate genre. It pays 3 ¢ per word (to max $100). Word count: under 10,000 words. Please read full guidelines before submitting.

Submission Guidelines:

http://www.hd-image.com/aberrant_dreams/submission.htm

African Voices

This magazine was founded in 1992 in New York. It is a non-profit organization dedicated to fostering cultural under-standing and awareness through literature and the arts. The magazine has published more than 600 new creative voices in poetry, fiction and prose.

African Voices is one of only a few institutions to successfully publish a literary magazine and provide innovative programming in arts and education.

Well worth spending some time looking at their innovative ideas for involving children in literature.

Website: http://www.africanvoices.com

Alchemy

This is a magazine of fantasy fiction. It is looking for fantasy stories up to 8,000 words; pays 5 ¢ per word, on publication; hard copy submissions only to: Steve Paschenick, Editor, Alchemy, PO Box, 380264, Cambridge, MA, 02238, USA. Have a look at some short story and novel extracts at

http://www.sfsite.com/iv/fictional.htm and their general site at www.sfsite.com/12b/al190.htm

American Short Fiction Magazine

American Short Fiction accepts submissions of any length all year round; simultaneous submissions are accepted on the condition that the author notifies them immediately, by telephone or e-mail, if the manuscript is accepted for publication elsewhere.

Submit stories online. They pay $300 to $500 depending on the length of the manuscript. ASF also holds a short story contest, with a $1,000 prize, each fall.

What will attract them: precise and vivid use of detail and your language skills.

What will repel them: stilted, expository dialogue.

N.B. Research the magazine before submitting to it.

For more information:

See their website: www.americanshortfiction.org, or email the editors: editors@americanshortfiction.org

Asimov's Science Fiction Magazine

They are looking for 'character oriented' stories; those in which the characters, rather than the science, provide the main focus for the reader's interest. Serious, thoughtful, yet accessible fiction constitute the majority of their purchases, but there's always room for the humorous as well. Borderline fantasy is fine, but no Sword & Sorcery. They are not interested in explicit sex or violence. A good overview would be to consider that all fiction is written to examine or illuminate some aspect of human existence, but that in science- fiction the backdrop you work against is the size of the Universe. http://www.asimovs.com/2011_01/index.shtml

The Antioch Review

This is one of the oldest, continuously publishing literary magazines in America. They publish fiction, essays, and poetry from both emerging as well as established authors.

Check out their website for more details:

http://review.antioch.edu

Alfred Hitchcock Mystery Magazine

As this is a mystery magazine, the stories they buy will fall into that genre in some sense or another. They are interested in nearly every kind of mystery: stories of detection of the classic kind, police procedurals, private eye tales, suspense, courtroom dramas, stories of espionage, and so on. They ask only that the story be about a crime (or the threat or fear of one). They sometimes accept ghost stories or supernatural tales, but those also should involve a crime.

They do not accept email submissions.

It will obviously be useful to read one or more issues of *AHMM* to give you an idea of the kind of fiction they buy. For a sample copy, send a cheque made out to *AHMM* for $5.00 to:

Alfred Hitchcock Mystery Magazine
Attn: Sandy Marlowe
6 Prowitt St.
Norwalk, CT 06855.

Submissions should be sent to:
Dell Magazines
AHMM
267 Broadway
4th Fl.
New York, NY 10007-2352

They prefer that stories are shorter than 12,000 words. [In fact, most of the stories in the magazine are considerably shorter than that so it would obviously be better if you submitted stories well below the 12,000 wordage.] They are looking for fiction that is fresh, well told, absorbing and has not been previously published elsewhere.

N.B. Don't send them stories based on actual crimes or other real-life events. They only want fiction.

Website: http://www.themysteryplace.com

The Bellingham Review

A small American literary magazine. It pays $15 a printed page for literary fiction and non-fiction up to 9,000 words; they also publish poetry. It pays on publication. Submissions: to Fiction or Non-fiction Editor, Bellingham Review, Western Washington University, Mail Stop 9053, Bellingham, WA, 98225, USA.

Website: www.wwu.edu/~bhreview

Blackgate Fantasy Magazine

Black Gate publishes epic fantasy fiction at all lengths, including novel excerpts, as well as articles, news and reviews. They're looking for adventure-oriented fantasy fiction suitable for all ages, as long as it is well written and original.

They want to attract younger readers to the genre, and advertise themselves as a family-friendly publication, so don't send them material that is sexually explicit or gratuitously violent.

It accepts both electronic and hard copy submissions. Their submission address is:

New Epoch Press

Submissions Dept

815 Oak Street

St. Charles, IL 60174

Their email address is submissions@blackgate.com

Website: http://www.blackgate.com

Carve Magazine

Carve is seeking the highest quality literary short stories. They want emotional jeopardy, soul, and honesty. As usual, they recommend reading their most current issues to get an idea of what they're looking for.

They ask writers to submit only one short story and wait for a response before sending another. They do not accept genre fiction or poetry. However, they will accept a novel excerpt if it stands alone as a short story and accept simultaneous submissions.

Although they obviously don't accept every story, they offer comments or suggestions on some stories they return if they think they have potential. Because of this, their response time may be lengthy.

At the time of print, payment varies between $20 - $50 for a story. All authors are paid the same rate per story within a single issue.

They accept email submissions at submissions@carvezine.com and postal submissions at: Carve Magazine, P.O. Box 701510, Dallas, TX 75370

Clarkesworld Magazine

This is an online science fiction and fantasy magazine that publishes short fiction, interviews, articles and audio fiction on a monthly basis. Word Limit: 1000-8000 words (preferred length is 4000)

Pay Rate: 10¢ per word up to 4000 words, 5¢ per word after that. [At the time of print.]

They ask for First World Electronic Rights (text and audio), First Print Rights (author must be willing to sign 100+ chapbooks), and non-exclusive Anthology Rights for Realms; the yearly *Clarkesworld Anthology*.

Stories need to be easily read for on-screen reading. I.e. Very long paragraphs or typographical trickery will work against you.

Science-fiction need not be "hard" SF, but rigor is appreciated. Fantasy can be folkloric, medieval, contemporary, surreal, etc. Horror can be supernatural or psychological, so long as it is frightening. Profanity, gore and sexuality are allowed if they are deemed vital to the story.

http://clarkesworldmagazine.com

Fantasy and Science Fiction Magazine

They are obviously looking for stories that will appeal to science fiction and fantasy readers. The SF element may be slight, but it should be present. They prefer character-oriented stories. They receive a lot of fantasy fiction, but never enough science fiction or humour. Do not send them a query, but send the entire story. They publish fiction up to 25,000 words in length. Please read the magazine before submitting. A sample copy is available for $6.00 in the US and $8.50 elsewhere (to NJ address).

They do not accept simultaneous or electronic submissions. Please type your manuscript on clean white bond, double spaced, with one inch margins. For a good article on standard manuscript preparation, see www.sfwa.org/2008/11/manuscript-prepa-ration/. Put your name on each page, and enclose a self-addressed, stamped envelope. Writers from abroad are encouraged to send recyclable manuscripts with a letter-sized SASE and an International Reply Coupon or 95 ¢ in US postage (75 ¢ to Canada and Mexico). You can obtain information on how to place an international order by going to faq.usps.com and enter "postal store – International Orders" in the search box then the top entry in resulting list of links provides the necessary details.

They prefer only one submission from a writer at a time. Allow 8 weeks for a response. Please write and enclose a self-addressed stamped envelope if you have any questions.

Payment is 6-9 ¢ per word on acceptance. They buy first North American and Foreign Serial Rights and an option on Anthology Rights. All other rights are retained by the author.

Send story submissions as well as orders for sample copies to Gordon Van Gelder, Fantasy & Science Fiction, P.O. Box 3447, Hoboken, NJ 07030.

Freight Stories
Their logo: "The best new fiction on the web. Or anywhere else, for that matter."

Freight Stories seek to publish the finest contemporary fiction.

Send them stories, stand-alone novel excerpts, and novellas. They do not publish work that exists solely for readers of romance, mystery, crime, and erotica. However, they will consider works of literary fiction that explore the lives of 'rich characters'. Fiction of all lengths and styles is welcome. They would like your work to be driven by the exploration of the lives of believable, compelling characters that help to illuminate, or in some way enrich, readers' perspectives.

http://www.freightstories.com

Fried Fiction

This site is for serial fiction only. The episode does not need to tell a complete story, but should leave the reader wanting more.

They are looking for well written, open ended stories (or serials) of any genre, with a few exceptions, such as fan fiction (which may infringe upon copyrights) and erotic fiction.

Submissions are currently accepted over e-mail, although an online form is forthcoming. Please submit the following in .rtf or .txt file format to submissions@friedfiction.com, with the header "Fiction Submission"

Here is what they want: your name / pen name; a brief bio (about 50 words); a synopsis of the serial (around 100 words); written in any of these genres: literary, sci-fi, fantasy, horror, romance, western, historical, spy, military, crime, mystery, thriller or adventure. The first episode should be under 1000 words

Only the author's initial submission is required to pass through a selection process. Once approved, the author may add new episodes at their own pace, (through the web interface).

The initial selection process for an author is intended to ensure that the writing is of a high quality. Significant grammatical errors will result in rejection. Stories should have a strong focus on characters, and abide by the general rules of style (I.e. show, don't tell; minimize passive verbs, etc). Please do not submit stories that are mostly dialogue. This journal does not edit stories in the traditional manner, and prefers writers who are able to self-edit their work.

Payment rate: They offer 25 dollars for the first episode of a series (1000 words). There is currently no payment for additional episodes.

Expect a reply within two to six weeks.

http://www.friedfiction.com

Ghostly Encounters

If you, or a family member, have ever had a haunting experience, this magazine could be interested. Stories [1,000-2,000 words] are needed for a collection of personal ghost tales, *'Ghostly Encounters: Personal Experiences with the Supernatural'*. Contributors will be paid $50 on publication plus a copy of the book. No more than two photos per story; no fiction. Include sae and IRCs if you want your submission returned, and also your e-mail contact in addition to mailing address Ghostly Encounters, PO 1 600745, Dallas, TX 75360-0: USA.

Glimmer Train

They welcome the work of established and upcoming writers and have no reading fees for standard story submissions, only for their competitions. However, the monetary award paid to competition winners is more substantial than the already good $700 payment for accepted standard submissions, and agents are on the lookout for competition winners.

They appreciate work that is both well written and emotionally engaging. Log on to their web-site for all the information you need to submit a story. http://www.glimmertrain-press.com

Hennen's Observer

Hennen's Observer is a literary magazine and website that

supports writers taking their first steps in the world of publishing. They offer writers the opportunity to display their work on an international level and to compensate the best talent for their creative donations.

Hennen's Observer has two parts: the website and the magazine. The website is a free forum for everyone who wishes to submit his or her material. 'Everything goes' in this arena, but remember others will be reading your work so even though the site states that online material will be of varying genre and quality, make sure that your work is polished before sending any of it out. An agent could just be browsing the site! At the time of print, they pay $75 for poems and negotiate for short stories.

Not only does *Hennen's Observer* create new opportunities for writers, poets, and artists to establish themselves, but they also support "Reading is Fundamental". Founded in 1966, RIF is the oldest and largest children's and family nonprofit literacy organization in the United States. To learn more, go to www.rif.org.

Website: http://hennensobserver.com

Icarus

The Magazine of Gay Speculative Fiction. *Icarus* publishes speculative fiction and sci-fi stories that feature gay male protagonists. They publish stories that feature the fantastic: from magical realism to hard SF to horror. They have published work by Tanith Lee, Lee Thomas, Sandra McDonald, and Tom Cardamone.

Payment ranges from Token [Under 1 US cent per word] to Semi-pro payment. [1 – 4.9 US ¢ per word.]

More info at: http://www.lethepressbooks.com/icarus

Kinships

Accepts fiction [7,500 words max] non-fiction [3,000 words max]. Pay starts a 1c [US] per word.

Postal submissions to: Senior editor, c/o Kinships, 1213 Plum Drive East, Ferdinanda Breach, FL 32034, USA.

The Missouri Review

This was founded in 1978 and is a highly-regarded literary magazine. It states on their website: "For the past twenty-five years we have upheld a reputation for finding and publishing the very best writers first." They are based at the University of Missouri and publish four issues each year. Each issue contains new fiction, poetry and essays. It also runs a writing prize. [See prizes]

Fiction: The site recommends that writers familiarize themselves with fiction from previous issues before submitting. It publishes humorous and literary short stories between 2,000 and 7500 words long at the time of print. It pays $30 per printed page. However, there is a fee for online submissions of $3.

Snail mail is free at:

Editor

The Missouri Review

357 McReynolds Hall

University of Missouri

Coumbia, MO 65211

Check the website for more details at

http://www.missourireview.org/main_info/guidelines.php

Massachusett's Review.

They seek a balance between established writers and promising new ones and are interested in various material of vitality relevant to the intellectual and aesthetic questions of our time. They have a broad appeal. Their commitment is regional, but not provincial. Payment $50 per story. Wordage: up to 8,000 words.

http://www.massreview.org

Paris Review

The Paris Review does not accept emailed submissions. Short stories should be sent by mail to the Fiction Editor at the following address:

The Paris Review,

62 White Street.

New York, NY 10013

All submissions must be in English and previously unpublished. Simultaneous submissions are acceptable as long as they are notified immediately if the manuscript is accepted for publication elsewhere. Be sure to include phone and [if possible] e-mail contact information. Please submit only one story manuscript at a time. They suggest that you read several issues of *The Paris Review* to get a feel for the sort of story the magazine publishes.

http://www.parisreview.com/

Public House Press

At the time of print, they are looking for writers in the following areas - fiction, creative non-fiction, alternative travel, bizarre and experimental, prophecies, humour and spoken word CDs. Please send all submissions to their PO Box. Do not send submissions via email. Attn: Literary Contest, Public House Press, P.O. Box 640409, San Francisco, CA 94164.

Website: www.publichousepress.com

One Story

One Story is an on-line literary magazine that contains only one story which is only available by subscription approximately every three weeks.

It is seeking literary fiction that is between 3,000 and 8,000 words. The stories can be any style and on any subject as long as they are good. They are looking for stories that leave readers feeling satisfied and are strong enough to stand alone.

One Story is offering $100 and 15 contributors copies for First North American Serial Rights. All rights will revert to the author upon publication.

It is looking for previously unpublished material. However, if a story has been published in print outside of North America, it will be considered. No stories previously published online will be accepted.

Website: http://www.one-story.com

SDO Fantasy

Is an ezine magazine at the literary end of the market. All issues are themed so check out the website for the list and the guidelines at: http://www.sintrigue.org/fantasy/index.html. Their definition of fantasy is far wider than wizards and dragons. Read some of the work on the site. They refuse to accept work in the body of an e-mail; you must attach your story, e-mail submissions: editor@sintrigue.org

Short Story America

An incredibly useful and interesting site for readers and writers of the short story genre. Every Friday, *Short Story America* publishes a new short story for readers to enjoy. This site is free to its members and obviously if you are writing short stories, you should also be reading them.

In addition to the stories, it provides networking opportunities for authors, teachers, publishers and readers in America who want to be socially and intellectually connected with others who appreciate stories. Original SSA stories, or from the library of classic short stories are available on the site. *Short Story America* also publishes an annual print volume of short stories, featuring the 52 weekly stories published each year by SSA. Here is a website for writers all over the world to enjoy.

http://www.shortstoryamerica.com

Strange Horizons Fiction

They want good speculative fiction. If your story doesn't have a clear fantasy or science-fiction element, or at least strong speculative-fiction sensibilities, it's probably not for them.

They want to make the field of speculative fiction more inclusive; more welcoming to both authors and readers from traditionally underrepresented groups, so they're interested in seeing stories from diverse perspectives and backgrounds.

Here's what they are looking for: stories that have some literary depth but aren't boring; styles that are unusual yet readable; structures that balance inventiveness with traditional narrative. They want characters readers can care about and settings and cultures that they don't see all the time in speculative fiction.

If you've written a story that addresses political issues in complex and nuanced ways, then this is the outlet for you.

They prefer stories under 5,000 words long but will consider stories up to 9,000 words. [However, the longer the story, the less likely they are to be interested, so keep below the 5,000 word mark.]

They pay 7¢(US) per word, with a minimum payment of $50.

Website: http://www.strangehorizons.com

The New Yorker

Once you get a track record, contact the prodigious *The New Yorker Magazine*. It accepts literary and mainstream short stories between 1,000 and 7,500 words. Professional payment: 5 ¢ (US) or more a word.

Send a great pitch of your story to fiction@newyorker.com to fast-track yourself.

Website: http://www.newyorker.com/magazine

Tin House Magazine.

This magazine requires that writers buy a copy of the magazine before they submit any work. It requests that writers submit only one story and they do not accept multiple submissions. They try to respond within three months; however, in some cases this period may be longer. If you have not received a response from them within ninety days, they ask that you email them an inquiry.

Their reading period is September 1- May 31; submissions received after this date will be returned unread.

For postal submissions, write to: Tin House, PO Box 10500, Portland, OR 97210. Please enclose an SASE (include an IRC with international submissions), or they will not guarantee a response to or the return of your work.

For those of you who prefer submitting your work electronically please log onto their site, go to the submissions page and load up your story.

Website: http://www.tinhouse.com

The Threepenny Review

This literary Californian Review has some great short stories, poems and articles so would be worth subscribing to.

At the time of print, *The Threepenny Review* pays $400 per story or article, $200 per poem or Table Talk piece which is very good. This payment buys First Serial Rights for their print and digital editions. The copyright reverts to the author immediately upon publication.

Please note: they don't read submissions between July and December so don't submit anything then. It would be cheaper to use their online system to submit work rather than their postal address which you'll find on their website.

Website: www.thethreepennyreview

Venus Press

A new e-publisher which specializes in erotic fiction; both erotic romance and pure erotica. They publish all sub-genres, including fantasy, science fiction, suspense, historical, etc. The story must be engaging, with a solid plot and fully 'fleshed' characters. [Their words, not mine!] The publisher has new lines opening up, including its 'Sons of Zeus and Venus Rising', which asks for new twists to classic Greek myths. So if this sounds like you, log onto to www.venuspress.com and check out the submission guidelines.

Zoetrope: All-Story

This is a quarterly literary publication founded by Francis Ford Coppola in 1997 to explore the intersection of story and art, fiction and film. The magazine is devoted to publishing the best new short fiction and one-act plays. It has received every major story award, including the National Magazine Award for Fiction, while publishing today's most promising and significant writers.

Log onto http://www.all-story.com for more details.

Canadian Outlets

The Antigonish Review

For forty years, *The Antigonish Review* has consistently published fine poetry and prose by emerging and established writers.

It features poetry, fiction, reviews and critical articles from all parts of Canada, the US and overseas, using original graphics to enliven the format.

Payment for fiction is $100,00 plus 2 copies of the issue in which the story appears.

The journal will not accept submissions between June 1 – September 30 in any year so make sure you don't waste money by sending your story during the wrong months.

At the time of print, all submissions outside of those dates should be sent between to:

Bonnie McIsaac, Office Manager

P.O. Box 5000,

St. Francis Xavier University,

Antigonish,

Nova Scotia

Canada

B2G 2W5

Telephone: (902) 867-3962

Phone: (902) 867-5563

Website: http://www.antigonishreview.com

Broken Pencil

Want original stories that have never before published before. Word lengths of between 50 - 3,000 words. The editor asks you to put your name, contact info, story title and word count, and a short bio in the body of the email. Please send the story itself as an attachment in Microsoft Word format, not in the body of the email. Your name, the title of the story, and approximate word-count should also be written at the top of at least the first page of the story, if not on every page. Her favourite font size and style is 12-point Times New Roman and she asks writers to double space their work as it is much easier to read.

This site contains some valuable advice to writers. Here is what the editor says:

"What it comes down to is, your story needs to be not only awesome but also fit the style and theme of *Broken Pencil*. We like it weird. We want it to mean something — if we can see that it meant something to you when you wrote it, then it's going to mean something to us when we read it. We want to taste your blood on the page. We want your story to hurt us when we read it, we want to see that it hurt you to write it; we're a bit sadomasochistic in our literary tastes here at BP, apparently. Maybe that's why we take such perverse pleasure in encouraging all you writers out there to take a chance."

If you think your style is painful enough for *Broken Pencil*, here's where to send your polished story.

Email submissions to fiction@brokenpencil.com

Their payment ranges from $30 to $300 depending on what kind of story/article you are writing.

The Capilano Review

The Capilano Review has a long history of publishing new and established Canadian writers and artists who are experimenting with or expanding the boundaries of conventional forms and contexts. International writers and artists appear in their pages too. Now in its 38th year, the magazine continues to favour the risky, the provocative, the innovative, and the dissident.

Please note the following essential details when submitting a story to this Review:

Enclose a self-addressed envelope. If you are submitting work from outside Canada, please include an international reply coupon or Canadian stamps.

Print your name and address on the manuscript.

Ensure that your story is not over 6,000 words.

Post a hard copy to them as they do not accept submissions by email or on disk.

They publish with First North American Serial Rights and contributors are paid $50 per published page to a maximum of $200.

The Capilano Review

2055 Purcell Way

North Vancouver, BC

V7J 3H5

contact@thecapilanoreview.ca

Website: http://www.thecapilanoreview.ca/submissions.php

The Dalhousie Review

This Review likes spellings that can be seen in *The Canadian Oxford Dictionary*. *E.g.* 'catalogue,' 'colour,' 'program,' 'travelling,' 'theatre,' etc. However, writers are encouraged to follow whatever canons of usage might govern the particular work in question, and to be inventive with language, ideas and form. Works of fiction should in general not exceed 5000 words.

All submissions should be made in hard copy only, sent by post to:

The Dalhousie Review

Dalhousie University

Halifax, Nova Scotia

B3H 4R2 Canada

Please include an email address, which they will use to notify you of their decision. If you would prefer notification by post, or return of a manuscript that they do not use, please include a self-addressed envelope and return postage in Canadian stamps or International Reply Coupons.

If your story is accepted for publication, the author should supply an MS Word file, sent by email attachment to dalhousie.review@dal.ca. Authors will also be asked to supply a brief (2–3 line) biographical note.

They discourage simultaneous submissions. Authors of accepted material are required to provide their assurances that the work has been neither published nor accepted for publication elsewhere. They accept submissions year-round and try to respond within 3–9 months. However, if the volume of submissions is high, this could be longer.

> http://dalhousiereview.dal.ca/subm1.html

Descant

It considers submissions of poetry, short stories, novel excerpts, plays, essays, interviews, musical scores and visual presentations. Standards for acceptance are high. They receive a large number of submissions every month so please send only your best, carefully edited work. No submission may be under consideration by another publisher, nor can it have been previously published. Please note that it can take up to 12 months to hear back from them regarding your submission.

Submissions must be typed, double-spaced on one side of the page, with ample margins. Good quality photocopies or computer printouts are acceptable. On your envelope please print your full name, type of submission and complete address.

They do not accept email submission or links to websites.

Descant pays a $100 honourarium upon publication.

Submissions to:

Descant Magazine

P.O. Box 314, Station P

Toronto, ON

M5S 2S8

info@descant.ca

Website: http://www.descant.ca

The Fiddlehead

The Fiddlehead is open to good writing in English from all over the world; they are looking for freshness and surprise. Their editors are always happy to see new unsolicited works in fiction and poetry. Work is read on an ongoing basis, but their acceptance rate is only around 1-2%. [They state that they are famous for their rejection notes so this is not an outlet for the faint-hearted!). Response time is typically from three to nine months. Apart from their annual contest about which you will find details on their website, they have no deadlines for submissions.

If you are serious about submitting to *The Fiddlehead*, you should subscribe or read an issue or two to get a sense of the journal. Contact them if you would like to order sample back issues ($10-$15 plus postage).

Requirements for submissions are similar to those for other literary journals:

All unsolicited submissions should be unpublished, original works.

No faxed, emailed submissions accepted. Please do not send CDs, DVDs, etc.

Please include a cover letter with contact information (including your email address, if you have one), the title(s) and genre of the work(s) you are submitting and one to three lines of biographical information about your writing career.

All submissions should be typed/word-processed, spell-checked, double-spaced and paginated. Please put your name on every page of your submission.

Please only submit in one genre at a time.

A short fiction submission should be under 4,000 words. Please send only one short fiction submission at a time.

Pay is approximately $40 per published page, plus two complimentary copies of the issue with your work.

The Fiddlehead buys First Serial Rights; copyright remains with the author.

Submissions to:
Fiction Editor
The Fiddlehead
Campus House 11 Garland Ct
UNB PO Box 4400
Fredericton NB E3B 5A3
Canada
fiddlehd@unb.ca
Website: http://www.lib.unb.ca

Grain Magazine

Grain Magazine is an internationally acclaimed literary journal that publishes engaging, surprising, eclectic, and challenging writing and art by Canadian and International writers and artists. It is published four times per year.

It has a nine-month reading period; September 1st to May 31st. Manuscripts postmarked and/or received between June 1st and August 31st will not be read. If you have work currently under consideration by *Grain*, please do not submit again until you have received a response to that submission. It does not accept email submissions.

Payment: All contributors, regardless of genre, are paid $50 per page to a maximum of $225, plus 2 copies of the issue in which their work appears.

Rights: *Grain* purchases First Canadian Serial Rights only. Copyright remains with the writer or artist.

Send Submissions To
Grain Magazine,
PO Box 67, Saskatoon,
SK, S7K 3K1, Canada
Email: grainmag@sasktel.net
Website: http://www.grainmagazine.ca

Room Magazine

Canada's oldest literary journal run by and about women. *Room* is a space where women can speak, connect, and showcase their creativity. Each quarter they publish original, thought-provoking works that reflect women's strength, sensuality, vulnerability, and wit.

They now welcome submissions of prose and poetry in English from women outside Canada.

It is committed to discovering new talents and they will read new-comers and experienced writers alike. However, if you have writing credits, don't forget to mention the following details in your cover letter:

where you've published previously; any contests you've won; any grants you've been awarded; any writing programs you've attended; any prizes you've won; any full-length book manuscripts you may currently have under contract or in circulation.

Please also include your name, address, phone number, and email address and an accurate word count of your piece.

Please make only one submission at a time and only submit quarterly.

Please submit 12-pt typed, double-spaced, single-sided pages of unpublished prose of no more than 3,500 words. They accept email and postal submissions. More details can be seen on their website:

http://www.roommagazine.com

Storyteller

Storyteller is a general fiction magazine. It publishes humour, adventure, mystery, drama, suspense, horror, SF and fantasy. Like other magazines and journals, it recommends that you read an issue or two to get a feel for what they publish.

Their editorial board chooses stories for their entertainment value and literary merit. They want characters their readers can care about, and 'who show who they are by what they do.'

Stories must be original works of fiction between 2,000 and 6,000 words. They occasionally accept reprints, but not from well-known magazines or webzines.

No simultaneous submissions. No electronic or faxed submissions.

Use standard story format [double-spaced, wide margins, etc.].

Your name, address, phone number, and e-mail address should appear in the upper left hand corner of the first page.

A brief cover letter is preferred, but is not a requisite.

At the time of print, they pay ½¢ per published word for original stories, ¼¢ per published word for reprints, plus 2 contributor copies.

More details on http://www.storytellermagazine.com

The Malahat Review

The Malahat Review, established in 1967, is among Canada's leading literary journals. Published quarterly, it features contemporary Canadian and international works of poetry, fiction, and creative non-fiction as well as reviews of recently published Canadian poetry, fiction, and literary non-fiction.

It reads all year to emphasize the contemporary nature of the writing it publishes. The best way to know what they are looking for is to order an issue at the address below: $14.45 in Canada (including shipping and postage), $16.45 for U.S. orders, and $17.95 for those from elsewhere.

Unsolicited submissions of short fiction may range in length from 1,200 – 8,000 words. Please specify the number of words in each story submitted.

It does not accept email submissions.

The Review purchases First World Serial Rights and upon acceptance pays $20 per published page, plus a one-year subscription. Copyright reverts to the author upon publication.

Submissions to:

Fiction Editor

University of Victoria

Box P.O. 1700, Stn CSC

Victoria, BC

V8W 2Y2

malahat@uvic.ca

http://www.malahatreview.ca

The New Quarterly: New Directions in Canadian Writing

'*The New Quarterly* is a wonderfully interesting and useful resource for anyone who is writing short fiction or for anyone interested in the Canadian fiction being written today.' Marilyn Gear Pilling

Their submission policy.

A single submission may include 1 short story, 3 poems, or 1 postscript story (under 3 pages).

Submissions must be typed and double-spaced with a word count.

Make sure you include your name, address, phone number and/or e-mail address in your cover letter as well as the titles of work submitted. Your name should also appear on the submission itself.

N.B. Please note that *The New Quarterly* **only** publishes Canadian writers, whether living at home or abroad. Please make your nationality clear in your cover letter if you live outside of Canada.

It does not consider e-mail submissions. However, the journal is happy to notify you by e-mail if you do not require return of your manuscript. Please indicate in your cover letter that you would like an e-mail response.

Include a short biographical note and, if you want your manuscript returned or prefer to receive their decision by post, a self-addressed stamped envelope. (Canadian postage or international postal reply coupons.).

They pay $250 for a short story on publication.

Send submissions to:

The Fiction Editor

The New Quarterly

c/o St. Jerome's University

290 Westmount Road North

Waterloo, ON, Canada

N2L 3G3

Website: http://www.tnq.ca

Prairie Fire

Prairie Fire is a quarterly magazine that looks like a book. Each issue is loaded with stories, poems and articles. It's a great way to read the latest from your favourite authors long before their next book is published.

The editors are committed to quality so they choose work chiefly because of its excellence. The writing in *Prairie Fire* may be by renowned authors like Jake MacDonald, Margaret Sweatman or Miriam Toews, or it may be you - a talented newcomer being published for the first time. They want good, solid writing that will engage the mind and spirit of readers. They accept short stories up to 10,000 words.

The editors enjoy variety which is why they publish a wide range of writing including poems, stories, personal essays, and interviews. They also publish the winners of their annual writing competitions.

Prairie Fire buys First North American Serial Rights only. Rights are reassigned to the author upon publication. Payment is made following publication and includes one free contributor's copy. The term 'page' refers to published page. They reserve the right to pay for only 3/4 page if any page occupies 34 lines or less; for only 1/2 page if 23 lines or less; for 1/4 page if 12 lines or less. The 'kill fee'* for material accepted in writing but subsequently not used is $25-$50.

* A 'kill fee' is a negotiated payment for a magazine or newspaper article that is given to the writer if their assigned story/article is 'killed'. I.e. cancelled. This is generally expressed as a percentage of the total payment. However, in this magazine it is a fixed rate.

On their site they state that they reserve the right to refuse payment for work which proves to have been previously published elsewhere, or which turns out to have been plagiarized. Commissioned writing and anything not covered by this rate sheet will be negotiated on an individual basis. These rates are subject to change without notice. (Electronic rates will be negotiated separately.)

They pay $50 for the first page; $45 for each additional page. Maximum fee is $500.

Submissions to:

Fiction Editor

423-100 Arthur St.

Winnipeg, MB

R3B 1H3

prfire@mts.net

http://www.prairiefire.ca

Qwerty

Fiction/Creative Non-Fiction/Reviews: max. 3,000 words Submissions should be: mailed in hard copy; typewritten, double-spaced; accompanied by a cover letter with your name, address, phone number, bio, and email address. It should be unpublished and not submitted simultaneously.

Submissions from outside Canada can opt to receive a reply via email (please mention in cover letter). If you would like a mail reply, you must include a sufficient number of International Reply Coupons to cover the return postage.

Send your submissions to:

Qwerty
c/o UNB English Dept.
PO Box 4400
Fredericton, NB
E3B 5A3
Canada
For inquiries, email: qwerty@unb.ca
Website: http://www.lib.unb.ca/Texts/Qwerty

Canadian Writer's Journal
There is a wealth of useful information for writers in this journal:
An extensive listing of the Canadian Writer's Contest Calendar;
Articles about Copyright Laws;
A very useful PDF guide called "The Writer's Studio Guide To Publishing in Literary Magazines and Entering Contests". I only found this guide after I'd spent hours and hours researching!]
Another amazingly useful page is called "Writers Beware" which highlights scams and pitfalls that can threaten writers. It has numerous articles on a host of subjects like the pitfalls of vanity publishing; being careful with predator agents who charge writers; the low-down on e-publishing, etc. There is far too much information to mention here so please spend some worthwhile time reading the invaluable information on this site.
http://www.cwj.ca/05-writer.htm

Here are a few more outlets to which you can sell your story in Canada, but there is no space to include detailed information on them all.
Queen's Quarterly
Queen's University
Kingston, ON
K7L 3N6
quarter@post.queensu.ca

http://www.queensu.ca

Subterrain Magazine
P.O. Box 3008, MPO
Vancouver, BC
V6B 3X5
subter@portal.ca
http://www.subterrain.ca

Taddle Creek
P.O. Box 611, Station P
Toronto, ON
M5S 2Y4
editor@taddlecreekmag.com
http://www.taddlecreekmag.com

West Coast Line
2027 East Academic Annex
Simon Fraser University
Burnaby, BC
V5A 1S6
wcl@sfu.ca
http://www.westcoastline.ca

Australian and New Zealand Outlets

Aurealis

This is a sci-fi/fantasy magazine that seeks to increase the profile of Australian sci-fi writing by producing a mass market magazine. The editors hope that their website brings Australian science-fiction and fantasy into the global SF community.

On their site they state that this magazine has provided a reliable market for established writers since it was launched in 1990. In 1995 it instituted the Aurealis Awards for Excellence in Australian Speculative Fiction.

Submission guidelines:

It is looking for science-fiction, fantasy or horror short stories between 2,000 and 8,000 words. All types of science fiction, fantasy and horror that are of a 'speculative' nature will be considered, but they don't want stories that are derivative in nature, particularly those based on TV series.

Stories do not have to be explicitly Australian, although they like to see some with Australian characterisation and background, provided the local element is not merely a self-conscious insertion into a standard plot.

Aurealis pays between $20 and $60 per 1000 words. Payment will be made soon after the publication of the issue containing your story. Minimum payment is $20.

More details can be found on: http://www.aurealis.com.au

Borderlands

Australian Sci-Fi, Fantasy and Horror

Borderlands is open to unsolicited submissions of Australian quality speculative fiction. I.e. Fiction with some elements of science fiction, fantasy or horror or related genres. This outlet is only open for Australian citizens, Australian born, or Australian resident.

They state that they are very flexible on the speculative (a hint of magic realism might be enough), somewhat flexible on the Australian, but not on the quality. They pay $25 for stories.

They prefer electronic submissions where possible, mailed to submissions@borderlands.com.au.

However, they also accept postal submissions. Send to:

Fiction Editor

P O Box 276,

Bayswater,WA 6933.

Australia.

All manuscripts sent will be deemed disposable, and will not be returned to the author.

Heat Magazine

Since its first appearance in July 1996, the Australian international literary magazine *Heat* has been received enthusiastically by readers, and applauded in the press for the quality of its writing. They state: "As both a magazine and a book, *Heat* is designed to travel across academic boundaries, across literary categories, across languages and cultures. It offers the variety of poetry and fiction, essays and reviews, art and photography."

Payment: 5 ¢ or more per word.

All contributions should be sent as hard copy, with stamped self-addressed envelope (or international reply coupon) to:

Heat Magazine

Fiction Editor

Writing & Society Research Group

University of Western Sydney

Locked Bag 1797

Penrith South DC NSW 1797

Australia

Website: http://giramondopublishing.com/heat

Island Magazine

This magazine publishes quality short stories, poetry, extracts from forthcoming novels, and articles and essays on topics of social, environmental and cultural significance.

Publication rates: the minimum rates paid for contributions to *Island* are $150 per short story.

Submissions must be typed with double spacing, preferably on A4 paper with letter-quality print. Please write on only one side of the page, with a wide margin at left and right, and with a name and address on each page.

Manuscripts must be accompanied by a stamped self-addressed envelope and not be longer than 2,500 words.

No email submissions please.

Postal address:

Island,

Fiction Editor

PO Box 210, Sandy Bay,

Tasmania 7006 Australia

Ph: (03) 6226 2325 Fax: (03) 6226 2172

E-mail: island.magazine@utas.edu.au

Landfall Literary Journal

Landfall contains literary fiction and essays, poetry, extracts from work in progress, commentary on New Zealand arts and culture. It is a journal that caters for work by New Zealand and Pacific writers or by writers whose work has a connection to the region in subject matter or location. Work from Australian writers is occasionally included as a special feature.

The editor is interested in new work that has not been published before. While many established names appear in *Landfall's* pages, the editor and *Landfall's* readers are always on the lookout for exciting work from new writers and artists. If you are a new writer, find copies of *Landfall* in bookshops and libraries to get a sense of what is published.

Many issues of this magazine have themes so if you are a New Zealand/Australian writer, check frequently on their website for information about upcoming issues. Unsolicited submissions will be considered for all issues, whether themed or 'Open House'.

Submission Guidelines:

Email submissions are preferred and should be sent as a .doc or .rtf file to landfall@otago.ac.nz

Hard copy submissions should be sent to Landfall, c/o Otago University Press, PO Box 56, Dunedin, and will not be returned unless they include a self-addressed envelope.

Include the author's name on each page of your submission, in the running head.

Prose contributors - please submit no more than three pieces per issue (unless the pieces are exceptionally short). Include word length of each piece below the heading on the first page. Preferred word length is up to 5,000 words.

All submissions will be acknowledged on receipt and must have a covering email/letter, providing full contact details, including email and postal addresses, and a brief biography of about 30 words.

If you do not receive an acknowledgement, email landfall@otago.ac.nz.

Landfall is published six-monthly. Deadlines for submissions are 10 January for the May issue and 10 June for the November issue.

Website: http://www.otago.ac.nz/press/landfall/index.html

Meanjin Magazine

This is Australia's second oldest magazine which turned 70 in December, 2010.

As usual, they recommend that writers study the magazine's style to see if their work would suit this outlet.

They pay contributors a minimum fee of $100 for prose. All authors are sent a detailed contract.

Submissions should be sent in hard copy with a covering letter including full contact details and a brief biographical note.

Feel free to send more than one example of your work, but be aware that they may not be able to read long or multiple submissions with the same care and attention as shorter selections. They do not impose word limits on submissions, but note that they rarely publish work over 5,000 words.

A stamped, self-addressed envelope or email address must be included with all submissions. If they choose to publish your work, they will request a copy sent by email as an attachment or, where that is not possible, on disk.

Please allow three months for a response to unsolicited pieces. Submissions should be sent to:

Meanjin
Fiction Editor
187 Grattan Street
Carlton, Victoria 3053
Australia
Website: http://meanjin.com.au

Narrative Magazine

They want previously unpublished manuscripts of all lengths, ranging from very short stories to complete book-length works for serialization. *Narrative* regularly publishes fiction, poetry, and nonfiction, including stories, novels, novel excerpts, novellas, personal essays, humor, sketches, memoirs, literary biographies, commentary, reportage, interviews, and features of interest to readers who take pleasure in storytelling and imaginative prose. They are looking for quality and originality of language and content. However, you have to pay $20 for their reading fee which is very unusual. What is also unusual - they don't charge readers for the magazine, only writers!

If you want to pay them to read your work, send it via email as they don't accept postal submissions. Please look at their submission guidelines as they are specific.

http://www.narrativemagazine.com/submission-guidelines

Snorkel Magazine

Snorkel is an online literary magazine with a special interest in bringing together the creative writings of Australians and New Zealanders, while also welcoming submissions from the wider International community.

Submissions to *Snorkel* are by email. Only previously unpublished work is considered. Send up to two short stories (word limit up to 3,000 words per piece) as attachments in either Microsoft Word or Rich Text Format, or as text included in the body of the email, to snorkel@snorkel.org.au.

Takahe Magazine

The Takahe Collective Trust is a non-profit organisation that aims to support emerging and published writers, poets, artists and cultural commentators.

Their submission guidelines:

Please include with all work submitted and/or queries about proposed work:

- a biography of maximum 40 words, no matter how often or how recently your work has appeared in the magazine;
- your email address;
- if mailing hardcopy, a self-addressed envelope of an appropriate size (two, if you're submitting poems and short fiction concurrently), with return NZ postage (or an international reply coupon (IRC) for overseas submissions). Queries or submissions without an SSAE (or IRC) or email address will not be responded to.

However, as they prefer email submissions, save some money by sending your story to: fiction@takahē.org.nz

Their submissions guidelines are quite strict so please log onto their website and read them carefully.

http://www.takahe.org.nz/submissions

Wet Ink Magazine

This is a magazine that's dedicated to publishing new and exciting writing and actually pays the writer! Inside each issue you'll find fiction, poetry and creative non-fiction, interviews, photography, book reviews and more. They publish new talent, as well as previously unpublished work by established authors.

Here are their writers' guidelines:

Please send no more than three submissions.

Only hard copies considered.

Include a cover sheet with the title of your work plus all contact details for each submission. [The cover sheet can be seen on line.]

Put your name on the cover sheet but NOT on the work.

Include date and word count.

Text should be double spaced in Times New Roman 12pt.

No word limit—although the longer a piece is, the more outstanding it needs to be to replace two or three shorter pieces.

They are also interested in shorter pieces (up to 500 words) that are funny, snappy, experimental or thought-provoking.

If your story is accepted, once it has been published, you are then free to submit that work elsewhere. However, *Wet Ink* asks writers to acknowledge previous publication by including the line "This story was first published in issue ... of Wet Ink".

If the editors want to publish your story you will be notified by email and asked to resend it as a MS Word document.

Please allow 4 months for a response. If you have not heard from them in that time your story has not been accepted.

Published stories are paid $70 for under 1500 words; $120 above 1,500 words. [I know which wordage I would aim for!]

Submissions to:

Wet Ink Magazine Inc

PO Box 3162

Rundle Mall
SA 5000
Australia
Enquiries can be directed to:
editor@wetink.com.au
Website: http://www.wetink.com.au

Kiwi Writers
If you are a New Zealand writer, you might be interested in joining a writing community that encourages anyone who is passionate about writing. They aim to support and promote New Zealand writers. If you're interested, log onto:

http://kiwiwriters.org

Other Outlets

The Barcelona Review

This is the Web's first electronic review of international, contemporary cutting-edge fiction in English/Spanish/Catalan multilingual format. (Original texts of other languages are presented along with English and Spanish translations as available.)

They are a small but ever-growing circle of mixed nationalities (Catalan, Spanish, French, American, English, and Scottish) who have come together over love of Barcelona, their home, and literature. Most of the people working on the review are directly or indirectly involved with the publishing business or with teaching literature. They read for a living and read a lot. The idea for the review came about from a desire to present, and in many cases introduce, their favorite authors to as large an audience as possible; especially authors well known within their own country or region, but not necessarily internationally.

Their common interest in writing lies somewhere in left field. What they are looking for is a well crafted story which has vitality - powerful, potent stories that immediately command attention and show stylistic and imaginative distinction; everything from cyberpunk to ultra-postmodern. In short, they are committed to publishing the very best material available in a wide variety of styles and techniques. New or little-known writers are presented along with known names.

Short Fiction: Submit one story at a time for consideration to the editor. Do not send a second piece until you have received a response to the first. Word length: 4,500 words max. Only previously unpublished work (print or online) accepted for reading. Simultaneous submissions are fine but please let them know immediately if accepted elsewhere.

To submit by e-mail: editor@barcelonareview.com. To retain punctuation and layout (including italics or any changes in font) send as a word processing document (Office [.doc], Apple Works converted to .doc, etc.) as an attached file. Use New Times Roman font, if available. Single space. Do not send a 'reader' document, i.e .pdf or HTML. Do not send the story in the body of the e-mail.

Fictionaut

"A literary community for adventurous readers and writers." It states on their site. They continue by saying "Whether you're a first-time writer or best-selling novelist, *Fictionaut* is a discerning, friendly place to show off your work. On *Fictionaut*, you can invite constructive criticism or post to attract a large, engaged audience of readers, editors, agents and publishers. Previously published work is acceptable, as is work in progress."

Could be a useful site to submit stories, but I wouldn't submit anything that isn't polished; especially if agents and publishers are likely to read your work.

Look at this link for more details: http://www.fictionaut.com

Istanbul Review

When Etkin Getir founded this literary magazine in 2005 his goal was to publish writers from all over the world and to culturally develop a strong literary community.

Here is what Gloria Mincock, the Editor-in-Chief, writes about the magazine: 'Over the years, we have published so many fabulous writers from different countries. The reputation of the magazine has been growing and we are starting to get more submissions from different countries. Susan Tepper (Assistant Editor) and I have kept Etkin's vision alive for the magazine. We never lose sight of what's important concerning the magazine.'

This is an online magazine so if you want your work to be viewed by people world-wide you can submit stories via their submissions page at http://www.ilrmagazine.com/submissions.

Pilvax

This is an on-line Hungarian review written in English. It originates from Budapest and they have a prevailing interest in work by writers living in or writing about Central or Eastern Europe. However, they are always on the lookout for quality writing from any source on any topic regardless of origin.

They are interested in poetry, short stories and personal essays under 5,000 words. They are also seeking translations of European writers into English. New translations and unpublished writers are very welcome.

Please log onto for more information

http://www.pilvaxmag.com/submit.html

Writers' Digest

A very useful site.

If you log onto this site you will find useful articles like 'Give Editors What They Want', interviews with Managing Directors of Literary Journals, through to what Small Presses are looking for. It also has useful sections on tips for writers, highlights what writing conferences are coming up, gives you exercises to stimulate your imagination and much more.

Well worth visiting.

http://www.writersdigest.com/GetPublishedCategory.

I've given you many useful websites, but there are many more, packed with useful information that will help you develop you own style of writing and that will also give you guidelines on how to submit your work. So please spend some time researching on your computer.

Remember you can sell the same story to a variety of markets and make money!

N.B. A word of support for writing magazines and journals. As a Writing Tutor, I realise the importance of outlets for writers, so how many magazines or journals do you subscribe to? It's vitally important for writers to subscribe to outlets which might publish their work. If you don't subscribe, you might find there are no outlets left for your own writing!

UK Short Story Competitions

Here is a small sample:
Smaller prizes

Cadenza Magazine

Cadenza is a twice yearly magazine, publishing vibrant, modern short stories, articles, poetry, interviews and markets of interest to fiction writers. It is A5 format, perfect bound with a glossy cover, and there are approx 80-90 pages of content. Editor Zoë King is looking for: short stories of up to 3,000 words submitted via their twice-yearly competitions. See their web-site: http://www.cadenza-magazine.co.uk for more details.

Dark Tales Flash Fiction

They have an ongoing contest with a deadline date of the first of the following months: September, November, January, March, May, July. For horror and speculative fiction. Maximum 500 words. First prize £25, second £5. Winner and runner-up - plus best short-listed - published in Dark Tales magazine. See website for full details: http://www.darktales.co.uk

Secret Attic

Runs a monthly short story competition and the winner is published in an e-booklet. They ask that you order a booklet before you enter a competition. More details on http://www.secretattic.com/competitions.htm

The Seventh Quark

Runs three separate competitions; a Quarterly Story Prize [2000-4000 words]; a Bi-Monthly Shorter Story Prize [under 2000 words], and a regular Frantic Flash Competition. Please see details of dates and entry fees on the website www.7thquarkmagazine.com or email seventhquark@tribe13.co.uk

Sunpenny Open Short Story Competition.

International entries accepted. Max 3000 words in any style, on any subject that conforms to good family values. [See website for full details and rules.] Entry fee: £3.00 per entry. Professional critique available for an additional £5.00 per critique. 1st Prize £200, 2nd Prize £100, 3rd Prize two books. More details on http://www.sunpenny.com/competitions/sscomp.html

Sunpenny Christian Short Story Competition

International entries accepted. Must have a distinct Christian message or theme. Max 3000 words in any style, on any subject that conforms to good family values and ratings. [See website for full details and rules.] Entry fee: £3.00 per entry. Professional critique available for an additional £5.00 per critique. Closing date: 30 September 2007. 1st Prize £200, 2nd Prize £100, 3rd Prize two books.

The Scribble Themed Competition

Max Length: 3000 words. Prizes: £100.00. £50.00. £25.00. Entry Fee: £4.00. [Cheques/postal orders to Park Publications.] Free entry for annual subscribers. The winning story will appear in their next issue of Scribble. Short-listed entries may also be considered for publication. Details: http://www.parkpublications.co.uk

The New Writer Annual Prose and Poetry Prizes

Short stories up to 4,000 words and serials/novellas up to 20,000 words on any subject or theme, in any genre [not children's]. Previously published material is not eligible for entry. Entry fees £4 per short story. Prizes: 1st prize £300, 2nd £200, 3rd £100. Novella: 1st prize £300. More details on http://www.thenewwriter.com/entryform.htm

Lichfield & District Writers Short Story Competition

First Prize: £125. Second Prize: £75. Third Prize: £25. Entry Fee: £3 for first entry, £2 each subsequent. Full details together with previous adjudicators' reports are available at: http://members.lycos.co.uk/Lichfield_Writers/index.htm

Monthly Writers' Forum Short Story Competition

Any genre, but stories must be original and previously unpublished. Aim for a word count between 1,500 to 3,000. Stories may embrace crime, mystery, romance, sport, humour, fantasy, erotica or science-fiction. The competitions are held monthly and there is also £1,000 for the best short story of the year. Monthly prizes of £250 for the best story published and two prizes of £150 for runners up. All stories not selected for publication are returned to authors with a grid assessment. Text should be type-written or word-processed, printed in double spacing. Entries should be accompanied with a short biography and colour photograph of the writer. Please submit a saved copy of the ms on disk as a Rich Text File [RTF] or Microsoft Word 5.1a [for Apple Macintosh]. Send complete M.S. and contact details to: Writers International Ltd, PO Box 3229, Bournemouth BH1 1ZS Tel: 01202 589828 Fax: 01202 587758 Website www.writers-forum.com

Wells Short Story Competition.

First Prize £500. 2nd Prize £200. 3rd Prize £100. Stories should be original and should be between 1800 and 2,000 words in length. This is one of the shorter short story competitions. Stories may be on any subject and should be typed double-spaced. There is no limit on the number of stories which may be submitted. More details on www.wlitf.co.uk/storyrules

LARGER PRIZES

Asham Award.

Britain's only prize for short stories by women.

In 2010 the prizes were: first prize: £1,000, second prize: £500, third prize: £300.

The runners up received £200 each, and had their stories published in a collection by Bloomsbury. Read Tobias Hill's online tutorial at http://www.ashamaward.com

Biscuit Publishing Short Story Prize

Enter a portfolio of three stories [any genre, including children's], each between 1,000 and 5,000 words long.

For more details, visit the Biscuit Publishing website
http://www.biscuitpublishing.com

BBC National Short Story Award

The BBC National Short Story Award celebrates the best of the contemporary British short story. Now in its fifth year, the Award continues to raise the profile of the short story. The inaugural Award went to James Lasdun for his short story "An Anxious Man"; in 2007 it was awarded to Julian Gough for his comic tale "The Orphan and the Mob"; and in 2008 the winner was Clare Wigfall for "Numbers" which appeared in her debut collection, "The Loudest Sound and Nothing", published by Faber in 2007.

This award offers a large prize of £15,000. As I've already stated, it was won in 2010 by David Constantine. Runner up was Jon McGregor for "If It Keeps Raining". He received £3,000. You can buy the book entitled 'The BBC National Short Story Award 2010' online from Comma Press. http://www.commapress.co.uk. By buying from this site, you not only support the short-listed writers, but the publisher who supported them in the first place. A double whammy!

Many more details of this award on the BBC website:

http://www.bbc.co.uk/radio4/features/national-short-story-award

Fish Publishing

This is an independent publishing company, founded in 1994. It aims to enable writers to have their work published in book format. The annual *Fish International Short Story Prize* has become an established event on the literary calendar, and numerous winners of the prize have gone on to publish many widely-acclaimed works. These include Eamonn Sweeney, Molly McCloskey, William Wall, Alex Keegan, Gina Ochsner, Suzanne Power and Martin Malone.

Fish Publishing also has other competitions - the One Page Story Prize, which is run annually, and the Short Histories Prize and the Unpublished Novel Award.

Postal address: Fish Publishing, Durrus, Bantry,

Co. Cork, Ireland. email: info@fishpublishing.com.

http://www.fishpublishing.com

Radio Short Stories

You have to be Irish to enter this competition.

RTÉ Radio 1 Short Story Competition runs in memory of Francis MacManus. This is an annual competition for original short stories for radio.

In the past, the competition offered prizes totalling €6,000 plus broadcast of all short listed stories on RTÉ Radio 1 and a commemorative trophy. The first three prizes were €3,000, €2,000 or €1,000.

A copy of the rules and an entry form can be downloaded form the website or by sending a stamped addressed envelope to:

RTÉ Radio 1 Short Story Competition, RTÉ Radio Centre, Dublin 4

The website includes an archive of dozens of short-listed

stories from three years of the competition all read by professional readers. Archived stories can be listened to for themselves or as a guide to what was best in radio short story writing as offered to this competition. [Please read these stories as they will be an invaluable guide to what this competition is looking for.]

The Crime Writer's Association Short Story Award

Your story needs to have been published before you enter for this award. First Prize: £1,500.

The winner and runner-up in 2010 were published in "Thriller 2: Stories You Just Can't Put Down", edited by Clive Cussler and published by MIRA Books, an imprint of Harlequin Mills & Boon.

The shortlisted stories (plus the judges' comments) were:

"A Calculated Risk" by Sean Chercover

Scuba diving takes on a new significance on the other side of the law. Subtly and deftly told with a menacing atmosphere.

"Boldt's Broken Angel" by Ridley Pearson

With one of the most memorable and compelling opening scenes, Boldt's Broken Angel follows Detective Boldt as he tracks down a twisted serial killer. A model thriller.

"Like a Virgin" by Peter Robinson (from The Price of Love)

A cold case brings back memories of a number of brutal murders and its repercussions. Elegantly written, containing many unforgettable images that comes back to haunt you.

"Killing Time" by Jon Land

Time is the enemy of a professional killer after a murder goes terribly wrong. Gruesome, but an intriguing, credible story.

"Protecting the Innocent" by Simon Wood

A stubborn love-struck protagonist is not averse to taking a little risk, but how far would you go for love? A tangled tale with horrific consequences for the love-struck characters.

More details on www.thecwa.co.uk

The Bridport Prize

The Bridport Prize is an annual International Creative Writing Competition for poetry and short stories. Max of 5000 words. 1st Prize = £5000; 2nd Prize = £1000; 3rd Prize = £500 + 10 supplementary prizes of £50. The closing date has gone for this year, but start writing one for next year now! However, be warned as the prizes are higher than average, many published writers enter this competition so the competition is tough.

The Jeffrey E. Smith Editors' Prize

The Missouri Review runs an annual Editors' Prize Contest in fiction, poetry, and essay, with a winner and three finalists named in each category. Length restrictions are 25 pages for fiction and essay, 10 pages for poetry. Winners are published in the following spring issue, plus each winner will receive a cash prize of $5,000 for fiction, poetry, and essay. Postmark deadline is October 1 each year. A $20 fee per submission includes a one-year subscription to the journal. See the website for more details.

http://www.missourireview.org/main_info/guidelines.php

The Sunday Times EFG Private Bank Short Story Award.

This is the largest short story prize in the world. In 2010, the prize was £25,000. Can you imagine getting that much money for writing one short story? No, don't rush out to post that letter of resignation! Don't tell your boss exactly what you think of him/her. I have some bad news. This competition is only open to authors with a previous record of publication in Creative Writing. [File the resignation letter under 'Sci-Fi Writing' and get published.]

In 2010, this award was won by one of New Zealand's most distinguished novelist and poet, CK Stead for his story "Last Season's Man". This story is set in Croatia where a young writer criticizes a hugely respected elder in an article, bruising the elder's ego and damaging his reputation among the intellectual community. However, there is a bitter-sweet ending.

In 2011, the prize is £30,000, but the five runners-up only receive £500 each which seems remarkably unfair as judges often argue about which writer should be the overall winner.

Website:

http://www.timesonline.co.uk/tol/system/topicRoot/The_Sun day_Times_EFG_Private_Ba

World Wide Short Story Competitions

Accenti Writing Contest

The Canadian Magazine with the Italian Accent

What a great strap line!

- Entries can be fiction, non-fiction or creative non-fiction.
- Entries must be previously unpublished and not under consideration by any other publication.
- Entries must be original and not a translation of a previously published work.
- Maximum length: 2000 words.

The contest is open to writers all over the world who write in English.

Entry Fee: $20

Prizes.

- Top prize: $1000.00 (CDN) and publication in Accenti.
- Second Prize: $250.00 (CDN) and publication in Accenti.
- Third Prize: $100.00 (CDN) and publication in Accenti.

Website: http://www.accenti.ca/writingcontest.asp

Fantastical Visions

The annual Short Fantasy Fiction Contest by Fantasist Enterprises is open to stories of a fantastical nature. This is a broad description, but basically they want magical stories, not technological. Entries must be between 4,000 and 10,000 words. 1st Prize = $125.00; 2nd Prize = $100.00; 3rd Prize = $75.00; runners up will be paid ½ cent a word. Winners and runners up will be published in an anthology. Email: contests@fanta sistent.com

More details on www.fantasistent.com

Global Short Story Writing Competition

If you are a writer with a hankering to have your writing exposed to an international audience then you may be interested in entering the *Global Short Story Competition*; a writing competition with the backing of acclaimed travel writer, Bill Bryson.

The *Global Short Story Competition,* a monthly writing competition run by Durham University in England, is open to writers from all over the world. The writing contest has been developed to showcase unknown writers and to build an international community of writers.

Each month a winning story, along with a highly commended entry, are selected for cash prizes - £100 GBP for the winner and £25 GBP for the runner-up. Winning stories of the *Global Short Story Competition* are displayed on the website. At the end of 12 months each winner is considered for a cash prize of £250 GBP and inclusion in an e-anthology.

In order to enter the writing contest online you need to be registered on the Global Short Story site. You can either pre-register or do so at the time that you submit your short story. The cost to enter the Global Short Story Competition is £5 GBP per story which can be paid electronically via Paypal. Postal entries are also accepted.

Submission Details

Entries must be not more than 2,000 words and may be on any theme and written in English. All writers must be aged 17 or over. All entries are limited to no more than 4 entries per individual.

The author retains copyright for short stories submitted however winning stories will be posted to the Global Short Story website.

Website: http://www.globalshortstories.net

Her Magazine Short Story Competition

A New Zealand magazine which runs a monthly short story competition. Entries must be original and previously unpublished. *Her Magazine* retains First Publication Rights for all winning entries for a period of six months.

Submission Guidelines

Entries to have a maximum of 1200 words and be double spaced

Each entry must be the author's original work and not been published before.

Submissions must be accompanied by a short biography of the writer.

Email submissions to: hermag@strettonpublishing.co.nz

There is no mention of monetary payment at the time of print. The 'payment' is publication in their magazine.

Life for Change

This is unusual writing contest in that you submit a short story and people vote for it. The author of the story with the most votes wins the money. There are no fees to submit. Currently payouts are $100.00 US. Website: www.lifeforchange.com

N.B. These competitions are on-going, so if you miss one dead-line, start writing for the next one.

Lorian Hemingway Short Story Competition.

Writers of short fiction are encouraged to enter the 2012 *Lorian Hemingway Short Story Competition*. The competition awards $2,000 in cash prizes. The literary competition is open to all writers whose fiction has not appeared in a nationally distributed publication with a circulation of 5,000 or more.

The Lorian Hemingway Short Story Competition was created in 1981 to support and encourage the efforts of writers who have not yet achieved major-market success and is organised by Ernest Hemingway's granddaughter.

See http://www.shortstorycompetition.com for more details.

The Glass Woman's Prize

This prize is run by the amazing Beate Sigriddaughter who is a German, living in Canada. She supports women writers from all over the world.

This is an annual competition awarded for a work of short fiction written by a woman. Length: between 50 and 5,000 words. The top prize for the ninth *Glass Woman Prize* award is US $500 and possible (but not obligatory) online publication; there will also be one runner up prize of $100 and one runner up prize of $50, together with possible (but not obligatory) online publication.

In addition, there are two further Anonymous Angel Awards of $100 each, thanks to a generous donation from a Canadian woman author who wishes to remain anonymous. [Isn't it wonderful when writers support each other?]

The theme of the story must be of significance to women. The criterion is passion, excellence, and authenticity in the woman's writing voice. Previously published work and simultaneous submissions are acceptable. Copyright is retained by the author.

Do have a look at this interesting website as you can read many of the winning stories on-line.

Website: http://www.sigriddaughter.com/GlassWomanPrize

The South African Literary Journal [New Contrast]

The South African Literary Journal is the oldest surviving literary magazine in South Africa. It is a journal that seeks to find new writing. It has been publishing prize-winning writers from the first issue in the Summer 1960 and continuing today. Here are some of the reasons why they'd like you to subscribe to this magazine:

'Literature is at the back of the queue when it comes to funding in South Africa, and it's you, the reader, who is keeping its flame alight. Your subscription helps guarantee the survival of creative expression.

For less than the cost of a paperback, you get four issues per year featuring the work of more than 30 writers, exposing you to voices that often go unheard in the hubbub of modern publishing.'

It publishes a wide spectrum of poetry, short stories, flash fiction and reviews.

Submissions to *New Contrast* may be sent email or post but emailed Microsoft Word documents are preferred.

Editor: ed@newcontrast.net.

Website: http://www.newcontrast.net

N .B. If these competitions aren't enough for you, check out this incredibly useful site which lists competitions for short story, play, screen and poetry writing throughout the whole year!

Ask About Writing. Website:

http://www.askaboutwriting.net/competitions

The Cask of Amontillado Story

by Edgar Allen Poe

The thousand injuries of Fortunato I had borne as I best could; but when he ventured upon insult, I vowed revenge. You, who so well know the nature of my soul, will not suppose, however, that I gave utterance to a threat. At length I would be avenged; this was a point definitively settled - but the very definitiveness with which it was resolved, precluded the idea of risk. I must not only punish, but punish with impunity. A wrong is un-redressed when retribution overtakes its redresser. It is equally un-redressed when the avenger fails to make himself felt as such to him who has done the wrong.

It must be understood, that neither by word nor deed had I given Fortunato cause to doubt my good will. I continued, as was my wont, to smile in his face, and he did not perceive that my smile now was at the thought of his immolation.

He had a weak point - this Fortunato - although in other regards he was a man to be respected and even feared. He prided himself on his connoisseurship in wine. Few Italians have the true virtuoso spirit. For the most part their enthusiasm is adopted to suit the time and opportunity - to practise imposture upon the British and Austrian millionaires. In painting and gemmary, Fortunato, like his countrymen , was a quack - but in the matter of old wines he was sincere. In this respect I did not differ from him materially: I was skilful in the Italian vintages myself, and bought largely whenever I could.

It was about dusk, one evening during the supreme madness of the carnival season, that I encountered my friend. He accosted me with excessive warmth, for he had been drinking much. The man wore motley. He had on a tight-fitting parti-striped dress, and his head was surmounted by the conical cap and bells. I was so pleased to see him, that I thought I should never have done wringing his hand.

I said to him - "My dear Fortunato, you are luckily met. How remarkably well you are looking to-day! But I have received a pipe of what passes for Amontillado, and I have my doubts."

"How?" said he. "Amontillado? A pipe? Impossible! And in the middle of the carnival!"

"I have my doubts," I replied; "and I was silly enough to pay the full Amontillado price without consulting you in the matter. You were not to be found, and I was fearful of losing a bargain."

"Amontillado!"

"I have my doubts."

"Amontillado!"

"And I must satisfy them."

"Amontillado!"

"As you are engaged, I am on my way to Luchesi. If any one has a critical turn, it is he. He will tell me -"

"Luchesi cannot tell Amontillado from Sherry."

"And yet some fools will have it that his taste is a match for your own."

"Come, let us go."

"Whither?"

"To your vaults."

"My friend, no; I will not impose upon your good nature. I perceive you have an engagement. Luchesi -"

"I have no engagement; - come."

"My friend, no. It is not the engagement, but the severe cold with which I perceive you are afflicted. The vaults are insufferably damp. They are encrusted with nitre."

"Let us go, nevertheless. The cold is merely nothing. Amontillado! You have been imposed upon. And as for Luchesi, he cannot distinguish Sherry from Amontillado."

Thus speaking, Fortunato possessed himself of my arm.

Putting on a mask of black silk, and drawing a roquelaire closely about my person, I suffered him to hurry me to my palazzo.

There were no attendants at home; they had absconded to make merry in honour of the time. I had told them that I should not return until the morning, and had given them explicit orders not to stir from the house. These orders were sufficient, I well knew, to insure their immediate disappearance, one and all, as soon as my back was turned.

I took from their sconces two flambeaux, and giving one to Fortunato, bowed him through several suites of rooms to the archway that led into the vaults. I passed down a long and winding staircase, requesting him to be cautious as he followed. We came at length to the foot of the descent, and stood together on the damp ground of the catacombs of the Montresors.

The gait of my friend was unsteady, and the bells upon his cap jingled as he strode.

"The pipe," said he.

"It is farther on," said I; "but observe the white web-work which gleams from these cavern walls."

He turned towards me, and looked into my eyes with two filmy orbs that distilled the rheum of intoxication .

"Nitre?" he asked, at length.

"Nitre," I replied. "How long have you had that cough?"

"Ugh! ugh! ugh! - ugh! ugh! ugh! - ugh! ugh! ugh! - ugh! ugh! ugh!'

My poor friend found it impossible to reply for many minutes.

"It is nothing," he said, at last.

"Come," I said, with decision, "we will go back; your health is precious. You are rich, respected, admired, and beloved; you are happy, as once I was. You are a man to be missed. For me it is no matter. We will go back; you will be ill, and I cannot be responsible. Besides, there is Luchesi -"

"Enough," he said; "the cough is a mere nothing; it will not kill me. I shall not die of a cough."

"True - true," I replied; "and, indeed, I had no intention of alarming you unnecessarily - but you should use all proper caution. A draught of this Medoc will defend us from the damps."

Here I knocked off the neck of a bottle which I drew from a long row of its fellows that lay upon the mould.

"Drink," I said, presenting him the wine.

He raised it to his lips with a leer. He paused and nodded to me familiarly, while his bells jingled.

"I drink," he said, "to the buried that repose around us."

"And I to your long life."

He again took my arm, and we proceeded.

"These vaults," he said, "are extensive."

"The Montresors," I replied, "were a great and numerous family."

"I forget your arms."

"A huge human foot d'or, in a field azure; the foot crushes a serpent rampant whose fangs are imbedded in the heel."

"And the motto?"

"Nemo me impune lacessit."

"Good!" he said.

The wine sparkled in his eyes and the bells jingled. My own fancy grew warm with the Medoc. We had passed through walls of piled bones, with casks and puncheons intermingling, into the inmost recesses of the catacombs. I paused again, and this time I made bold to seize Fortunato by an arm above the elbow.

"The nitre!" I said: "see, it increases. It hangs like moss upon the vaults. We are below the river's bed. The drops of moisture trickle among the bones. Come, we will go back ere it is too late. Your cough -"

"It is nothing," he said; "let us go on. But first, another draught of the Medoc."

I broke and reached him a flagon of De Grâve. He emptied it

at a breath. His eyes flashed with a fierce light. He laughed and threw the bottle upwards with a gesticulation I did not understand.

I looked at him in surprise. He repeated the movement - a grotesque one.

"You do not comprehend?" he said.

"Not I," I replied.

"Then you are not of the brotherhood."

"How?"

"You are not of the masons."

"Yes, yes," I said, "yes, yes."

"You? Impossible! A mason?"

"A mason," I replied.

"A sign," he said.

"It is this," I answered, producing a trowel from beneath the folds of my roquelaire.

"You jest," he exclaimed, recoiling a few paces. "But let us proceed to the Amontillado."

"Be it so," I said, replacing the tool beneath the cloak, and again offering him my arm. He leaned upon it heavily. We continued our route in search of the Amontillado. We passed through a range of low arches, descended, passed on, and descending again, arrived at a deep crypt, in which the foulness of the air caused our flambeaux rather to glow than flame.

At the most remote end of the crypt there appeared another less spacious. Its walls had been lined with human remains, piled to the vault overhead, in the fashion of the great catacombs of Paris. Three sides of this interior crypt were still ornamented in this manner. From the fourth the bones had been thrown down, and lay promiscuously upon the earth, forming at one point a mound of some size. Within the wall thus exposed by the displacing of the bones, we perceived a still interior recess, in depth about four feet, in width three, in height six or seven. It seemed to have been constructed for no especial use in itself, but formed merely the interval between two of the colossal supports of the roof of the catacombs, and was backed by one of their circumscribing walls of solid granite.

It was in vain that Fortunato, uplifting his dull torch, endeavored to pry into the depths of the recess. Its termination the feeble light did not enable us to see.

"Proceed," I said; "herein is the Amontillado. As for Luchesi-"

"He is an ignoramus," interrupted my friend, as he stepped unsteadily forward, while I followed immediately at his heels. In an instant he had reached the extremity of the niche, and finding his progress arrested by the rock, stood stupidly bewildered. A moment more and I had fettered him to the granite. In its surface were two iron staples, distant from each other about two feet, horizontally. From one of these depended a short chain, from the other a padlock. Throwing the links about his waist, it was but the work of a few seconds to secure it. He was too much astounded to resist. Withdrawing the key I stepped back from the recess.

"Pass your hand," I said, "over the wall; you cannot help feeling the nitre. Indeed it is very damp. Once more let me implore you to return. No? Then I must positively leave you. But I must first render you all the little attentions in my power."

"The Amontillado!" ejaculated my friend, not yet recovered from his astonishment.

"True," I replied; "the Amontillado."

As I said these words I busied myself among the pile of bones of which I have before spoken. Throwing them aside, I soon uncovered a quantity of building stone and mortar. With these materials and with the aid of my trowel, I began vigorously to wall up the entrance of the niche.

I had scarcely laid the first tier of my masonry when I discovered that the intoxication of Fortunato had in a great measure worn off. The earliest indication I had of this was a low moaning cry from the depth of the recess. It was not the cry of a drunken man. There was then a long and obstinate silence. I laid the second tier, and the third, and the fourth; and then I heard the furious vibrations of the chain. The noise lasted for several minutes, during which, that I might hearken to it with the more satisfaction, I ceased my labours and sat down upon the bones. When at last the clanking subsided, I resumed the trowel, and finished without interruption the fifth, the sixth, and the seventh tier. The wall was now nearly upon a level with my breast. I again paused, and holding the flambeaux over the mason-work, threw a few feeble rays upon the figure within.

A succession of loud and shrill screams, bursting suddenly from the throat of the chained form, seemed to thrust me violently back. For a brief moment I hesitated - I trembled. Unsheathing my rapier, I began to grope with it about the recess: but the thought of an instant reassured me. I placed my hand upon the solid fabric of the catacombs, and felt satisfied. I re-approached the wall. I replied to the yells of him who clamoured. I re-echoed - I aided - I surpassed them in volume and in strength. I did this, and the clamourer grew still.

It was now midnight, and my task was drawing to a close. I had completed the eighth, the ninth, and the tenth tier. I had finished a portion of the last and the eleventh; there remained but a single stone to be fitted and plastered in. I struggled with its weight; I placed it partially in its destined position. But now there came from out the niche a low laugh that erected the hairs upon my head. It was succeeded by a sad voice, which I had difficulty in recognising as that of the noble Fortunato. The voice said -

"Ha! ha! ha! - he! he! - a very good joke indeed - an excellent jest. We will have many a rich laugh about it at the palazzo - he! he! he! - over our wine - he! he! he!"

"The Amontillado!" I said.

"He! he! he! - he! he! he! - yes, the Amontillado. But is it not getting late? Will not they be awaiting us at the palazzo, the Lady

Fortunato and the rest? Let us be gone."

"Yes," I said, "let us be gone."

"For the love of God, Montressor!"

"Yes," I said, "for the love of God!"

But to these words I hearkened in vain for a reply. I grew impatient. I called aloud -

"Fortunato!"

No answer. I called again -

"Fortunato!"

No answer still. I thrust a torch through the remaining aperture and let it fall within. There came forth in return only a jingling of the bells. My heart grew sick - on account of the dampness of the catacombs. I hastened to make an end of my labour. I forced the last stone into its position; I plastered it up. Against the new masonry I re-erected the old rampart of bones. For the half of a century no mortal has disturbed them. In pace requiescat!

[Written in 1846]

The Secret Life of Walter Mitty

by James Thurber

"We're going through!" The Commander's voice was like thin ice breaking. He wore his full-dress uniform, with the heavily braided white cap pulled down rakishly over one cold gray eye. "We can't make it, sir. It's spoiling for a hurricane, if you ask me." "I'm not asking you, Lieutenant Berg," said the Commander. "Throw on the power lights! Rev her up to 8,500! We're going through!" The pounding of the cylinders increased: ta-pocketa-pocketa-pocketa-*pocketa-pocketa*. The Commander stared at the ice forming on the pilot window. He walked over and twisted a row of complicated dials. "Switch on No. 8 auxiliary!" he shouted. "Switch on No. 8 auxiliary!" repeated Lieutenant Berg. "Full strength in No. 3 turret!" shouted the Commander. "Full strength in No. 3 turret!" The crew, bending to their various tasks in the huge, hurtling eight-engined Navy hydroplane, looked at each other and grinned. "The old man will get us through," they said to one another. "The Old Man ain't afraid of Hell!"...

"Not so fast! You're driving too fast!" said Mrs. Mitty. "What are you driving so fast for?"

"Hmm?" said Walter Mitty. He looked at his wife, in the seat beside him, with shocked astonishment. She seemed grossly unfamiliar, like a strange woman who had yelled at him in a crowd. "You were up to fifty-five," she said. "You know I don't like to go more than forty. You were up to fifty-five." Walter Mitty drove on toward Waterbury in silence, the roaring of the SN202 through the worst storm in twenty years of Navy flying fading in the remote, intimate airways of his mind.

"You're tensed up again," said Mrs. Mitty. "It's one of your days. I wish you'd let Dr. Renshaw look you over."

Walter Mitty stopped the car in front of the building where his wife went to have her hair done. "Remember to get those overshoes while I'm having my hair done," she said. "I don't need overshoes," said Mitty. She put her mirror back into her bag. "We've been all through that," she said, getting out of the car. "You're not a young man any longer." He raced the engine a little. "Why don't you wear your gloves? Have you lost your gloves?" Walter Mitty reached in a pocket and brought out the gloves. He put them on, but after she had turned and gone into the building and he had driven on to a red light, he took them off again. "Pick it up, brother!" snapped a cop as the light changed, and Mitty hastily pulled on his gloves and lurched ahead. He drove around the streets aimlessly for a time, and then he drove past the hospital on his way to the parking lot.

... "It's the millionaire banker, Wellington McMillan," said the pretty nurse. "Yes?" said Walter Mitty, removing his gloves slowly. "Who has the case?" "Dr. Renshaw and Dr. Benbow, but there are two specialists here, Dr. Remington from New York and Mr. Pritchard-Mitford from London. He flew over." A door opened down a long, cool corridor and Dr. Renshaw came out. He looked distraught and haggard. "Hello, Mitty," he said. "We're having the devil's own time with McMillan, the millionaire banker and close personal friend of Roosevelt. Obstreosis of the ductal tract. Tertiary. Wish you'd take a look at him." "Glad to," said Mitty.

In the operating room there were whispered introductions: "Dr. Remington, Dr. Mitty. Mr. Pritchard-Mitford, Dr. Mitty." "I've read your book on streptothricosis," said Pritchard-Mitford, shaking hands. "A brilliant performance, sir." "Thank you," said Walter Mitty. "Didn't know you were in the States, Mitty," grumbled Remington. "Coals to Newcastle, bringing Mitford and me up here for a tertiary." "You are very kind," said Mitty. A huge, complicated machine, connected to the operating table, with many tubes and wires, began at this moment to go pocketa-pocketa-pocketa. "The new anesthetizer is giving way!" shouted an intern. "There is no one in the East who knows how to fix it!"

"Quiet, man!" said Mitty, in a low, cool voice. He sprang to the machine, which was going pocketa-pocketa-queep-pocketa-queep. He began fingering delicately a row of glistening dials. "Give me a fountain pen!" he snapped. Someone handed him a fountain pen. He pulled a faulty piston out of the machine and inserted the pen in its place. "That will hold for ten minutes," he said. "Get on with the operation." A nurse hurried over and whispered to Renshaw, and Mitty saw the man turn pale. "Coreopsis has set in," said Renshaw nervously. "If you would take over, Mitty?" Mitty looked at him and at the craven figure of Benbow, who drank, and at the grave, uncertain faces of the two great specialists. "If you wish," he said. They slipped a white gown on him; he adjusted a mask and drew on thin gloves; nurses handed him shining...

"Back it up, Mac! Look out for that Buick!" Walter Mitty jammed on the brakes. "Wrong lane, Mac," said the parking-lot attendant, looking at Mitty closely. "Gee. Yeh," muttered Mitty. He began cautiously to back out of the lane marked "Exit Only." "Leave her sit there," said the attendant. "I'll put her away." Mitty got out of the car. "Hey, better leave the key." "Oh," said Mitty, handing the man the ignition key. The attendant vaulted into the car, backed it up with insolent skill, and put it where it belonged.

They're so damn cocky, thought Walter Mitty, walking along Main Street; they think they know everything. Once he had tried to take his chains off, outside New Milford, and he had got them wound around the axles. A man had had to come out in a wrecking car and unwind them, a young, grinning garageman. Since then Mrs. Mitty always made him drive to the garage to have the chains taken off. The next time, he thought, I'll wear my right arm in a sling; they won't grin at me then. I'll have my right arm in a sling and they'll see I couldn't possibly take the chains off myself. He kicked at the slush on the sidewalk. "Overshoes," he said to himself, and he began looking for a shoe store.

When he came out into the street again, with the overshoes in a box under his arm, Walter Mitty began to wonder what the other thing was his wife had told him to get. She had told him, twice, before they set out from their house for Waterbury. In a way he hated these weekly trips to town-he was always getting something wrong. Kleenex, he thought, Squibb's, razor blades? No. Toothpaste, toothbrush, bicarbonate, carborundum, initiative and referendum? He gave it up. But she would remember it. "Where's the what's-its-name," she would ask. "Don't tell me you forgot the what's-its-name." A newsboy went by shouting something about the Waterbury trial.

... "Perhaps this will refresh your memory." The District Attorney suddenly thrust a heavy automatic at the quiet figure on the witness stand. "Have you ever seen this before?" Walter Mitty took the gun and examined it expertly. "This is my Webley-Vickers 50.80," he said calmly. An excited buzz ran around the courtroom. The Judge rapped for order. "You are a crack shot with any sort of firearms, I believe?" said the District Attorney, insinuatingly. "Objection!" shouted Mitty's attorney. "We have shown that the defendant could not have fired the shot. We have shown that he wore his right arm in a sling on the night of the fourteenth of July." Walter Mitty raised his hand briefly and the bickering attorneys were stilled. "With any known make of gun," he said evenly, "I could have killed Gregory Fitzhurst at three hundred feet *with my left hand*." Pandemonium broke loose in the courtroom. A woman's scream rose above the bedlam and suddenly a lovely, dark-haired girl was in Walter Mitty's arms. The District Attorney struck at her savagely. Without rising from his chair, Mitty let the man have it on the point of the chin. "You miserable cur!" ...

"Puppy biscuit," said Walter Mitty. He stopped walking and the buildings of Waterbury rose up out of the misty courtroom and surrounded him again. A woman who was passing laughed. "He said 'Puppy biscuit'," she said to her companion. "That man said 'Puppy biscuit' to himself." Walter Mitty hurried on. He went into an A&P, not the first one he came to but a smaller one farther up the street. "I want some biscuit for small, young dogs," he said to the clerk. "Any special brand, sir?" The greatest pistol shot in the world thought a moment. "It says 'Puppies Bark for It' on the box," said Walter Mitty.

His wife would be through at the hairdresser's in fifteen minutes, Mitty saw in looking at his watch, unless they had trouble drying it; sometimes they had trouble drying it. She didn't like to get to the hotel first; she would want him to be there waiting for her as usual. He found a big leather chair in the lobby, facing a window, and he put the overshoes and the puppy biscuit on the floor beside it. He picked up an old copy of *Liberty* and sank down into the chair. "Can Germany Conquer the World Through the Air?" Walter Mitty looked at the pictures of bombing planes and of ruined streets.

... "The cannonading has got the wind up in young Raleigh, sir," said the sergeant. Captain Mitty looked up at him through tousled hair. "Get him to bed," he said wearily. "With the others. I'll fly alone." "But you can't, sir," said the sergeant anxiously. "It takes two men to handle that bomber and the Archies are pounding hell out of the air. Von Richtman's circus is between here and Saulier." "Somebody's got to get that ammunition dump," said Mitty. "I'm going over. Spot of brandy?" He poured a drink for the sergeant and one for himself. War thundered and whined around the dugout and battered at the door. There was a rending of wood and splinters flew through the room. "A bit of a near thing," said Captain Mitty carelessly. "The box barrage is closing in," said the sergeant. "We only live once, Sergeant," said Mitty with his faint, fleeting smile. "Or do we?" He poured another brandy and tossed it off. "I never see a man could hold his brandy like you, sir," said the sergeant. "Begging your pardon, sir." Captain Mitty stood up and strapped on his huge Webley-Vickers automatic. "It's forty kilometers through hell, sir," said the sergeant. Mitty finished one last brandy. "After all," he said softly, "what isn't?" The pounding of the cannon increased; there was the rat-tat-tatting of machine guns, and from somewhere came the menacing pocketa-pocketa-pocketa of the new flame-throwers. Walter Mitty walked to the door of the dugout humming "Auprés de Ma Blonde." He turned and waved to the sergeant. "Cheerio!" he said...

Something struck his shoulder. "I've been looking all over this hotel for you," said Mrs. Mitty. "Why do you have to hide in this old chair? How did you expect me to find you?" "Things close in," said Walter Mitty vaguely. "What?" Mrs. Mitty said. "Did you get the what's-its-name? The puppy biscuit? What's in that box?" "Overshoes," said Mitty. "Couldn't you have put them on in the store?" "I was thinking," said Walter Mitty. "Does it ever occur to you that I am sometimes thinking?" She looked at him. "I'm going to take your temperature when I get you home," she said.

They went out through the revolving doors that made a faintly derisive whistling sound when you pushed them. It was two blocks to the parking lot. At the drugstore on the corner she said, "Wait here for me. I forgot something. I won't be a minute." She was more than a minute. Walter Mitty lighted a cigarette. It began to rain, rain with sleet in it. He stood up against the wall of the drugstore, smoking... He put his shoulders back and his heels together. "To hell with the handkerchief," said Walter Mitty scornfully. He took one last drag on his cigarette and snapped it away. Then, with that faint, fleeting smile playing about his lips, he faced the firing squad; erect and motionless, proud and disdainful, Walter Mitty the Undefeated, inscrutable to the last.'

[Written in 1939]

'Wanderer'

by Susan Gibb

'She daydreamed herself shrouded in her lover's arms, felt his warm weight pressing down on her. She imagined the musk scent of him, the soft brush of his mouth on her neck. She was oh-so-tired and her mind slipped like silk in the heat of a slow eastern wind.

People moved around her in a swirl of dry desert sand. The sun wept hot oil on her face. Out of hunger, she drifted away from the day, from the busy yet quiet murmur that floated with the perfume of jasmine in the air. In her mind she was weak from the lovemaking. Placid, and slow. Her fingers sought the curls of his hair, her mouth kissed the top of his brow. Her lips were parched and made no sound, her thirst as forgotten as the years under dreams of desire.

She stirred as someone shouted, slid back into reverie. Another voice sang in a high-pitched trill. She opened her eyes. In front of her just a few yards away stood her husband, her children pulling at his arms and crying words she barely could hear. Her daughter was sobbing, down on her knees, her small body straining against him. Her son stood firm, both of his hands gripping one of his father's. He stared into her face. She saw the conflict within him, his love stretched and hanging torn in the air. Tears locked for years inside her glass eyes crept up and spilled over, leaving large sparkling drops in the sand.

Her husband had never looked this frightening before. His anger was quiet. His anger was all in his face. She could not help but forgive him though he would never forgive her, she knew. Mahmoud stood steady and with a fling back of his arm, their daughter fell backward into the crowd.

She shut her eyes just as the first stone crushed into her jaw.'
[Written in 2010]

I have included this very short story to show you how powerful brevity can be. Susan Gibb's poignant and disturbing story won 'The Glass Woman's Prize' in 2010. It is only 321 words and yet it encompasses a whole world of culture and torn relationships.

Susan told me that she wanted to focus on the appalling dilemma of Sakineh Mohammadi Ashtiani whose life has been threatened by stoning for adultery. She wanted her brevity to 'pack a punch'. It certainly does in her story.

Isn't it fascinating how words and stories have changed since the 19th century?

Recommended Reading List

Here are some short story collections of writers who are well worth reading. Of course, there are many more writers for you to discover.

"*Don't Look Now and Other Stories*" by Daphne du Maurier. Penguin Classic. The first haunting story '*Don't Look Now*' was made into a memorable film starring Julie Christie and Donald Sutherland. This collection contains four other evocative stories which linger in the mind.

"*A Parisian Affair and other Stories*" by Guy de Maupassant. Penguin Classic. The stories are set in the nouveau riche Paris of society women, prostitutes and playboys. Dark, humorous stories which focus on the close relationships between lovers, siblings and ex-partners.

"*Short Stories*" by W. Somerset Maugham. Vintage Classic. Somewhat dated, but Maugham is still a fine spinner of tales. A wry, perceptive look at human foibles.

"*Flash Fiction*" edited by James Thomas, Denise Thomas and Tom Hazuka. Published in 1992 by W.W. Norton and Company. [You will discover Marlene Buono's fascinating story "*Offerings*" in this collection of very short stories.]

"*Tales of the Unexpected*" by Roald Dahl. First published in 1979 and still going strong. Republished by Penguin. Sixteen fascinating stories with startling twists. This is the man to read if you like surprises!

"*The Collected Short Stories of F. Scott Fitzgerald*". Penguin Classic. From his early stories of the glittering Jazz Age, through the lost hopes of the thirties to the last decade of his life. 'The Diamond as Big as the Ritz' is a fairy tale of unlimited wealth.

"*Matters of Life and Death*" by Bernard McLaverty. Vintage. The title says it all. Vivid, beautifully crafted stories.

"*The Blue*" by Maggie Gee. This is Gee's first short story

collection although she has published 10 acclaimed novels. Just shows you what an art form the short story can be. Subtle fables of everyday life; set against an intricate global backdrop.

"*Collected Stories*" by Gabriel Garcia Marquez. John Updike's quote from the New Yorker: "These stories are rich and startling in their matter and confident and eloquent in their manner...They are - the word cannot be avoided - magical."

"*The Tent*" by Margaret Atwood. Highly inventive tales from an incredibly gifted writer. This collection is a retelling of myths, fables and fairy tales, along with a couple of poems and fictional essays. If you like your mind stretched, here's the woman to stretch it for you.

"*Runaway*" by Alice Munro. Vintage. The stories focus on the power and betrayal of love, lost children and lost chances.

"The O Henry Prize Stories". 2006. Since 1919, the O. Henry Prize has meant excellence in literary short fiction. Named after William Sydney Porter [1862-1910] who was better known to readers as O. Henry. The prize was conceived in 1918 by his friends, members of the elite Twilight Club in order to honour him and strengthen the art of the short story. The selected stories encapsulate the human experience in both shocking and poignant terms.

"*The Collected Stories of Isaac Bashevis Singer*". Nobel Prize Winner, Isaac Bashevis Singer, is a master storyteller and readers will be well-rewarded for spending time with him. His stories are replete with the most profound insights into human nature and are told with dazzling skill.

"*The Stories of Eva Luna*" by Isabel Allende. This Chilean writer creates a treasure trove of stories; many of them showing us the power of love - how it can bring redemption or destruction. In "*Toad's Mouth*" we meet a powerful woman, who mesmerizes and enchants numerous men through her sexual prowess, but is tamed by a mysterious foreigner. While the final story is full of poignancy and mysticism. It describes the transformation of two people who have to face the past and accept the present. Allende is a writer who can weave spells through magical words and situations.

"How to Breathe Underwater" by Julie Orringer. Nine stories make up this award-winning debut. A recurring theme in the stories is the difficulty children have in communicating with the people closest to them. In *"Isabel Fish"* fourteen-year-old Maddy learns to scuba dive in order to heal her family after a terrible accident. These stories highlight the lack of communication between children and adults with compassion and wisdom.

READING ON LINE.

http://www.readbookonline.net

If you can cope with reading on line, the above link takes you to an amazing American site which contains about two thousand novels, non-fiction books, hundreds of short stories, poems, essays and plays.

Here's you'll find American, English and Irish Literature from the likes of William Shakespeare, Mark Twain, Charles Dickens, Oscar Wilde, Edgar Allan Poe and hundreds of others. This site is a treasure trove of words.

Its short story section features writers from all parts of the world and it shows you many different writing styles from the Spanish writer Pedro Antonio de Alarcon, the Norwegian writer Bjornstjerne Bjornson, the American writers Willa Cather, F Scott Fitzgerald, Kate Chopin and Nathaniel Hawthorne, the British writers Arthur Conan Doyle, George Elliot and Hector Hugh Monroe, the Russian writer Nikolai Vasilievi Gogol, the Irish writer James Joyce, the German writer Johann Wolfgang von Goethe, the French writer Victor Hugo, the Polish born writer Joseph Conrad and the Indian writer Rabinsdranath Tagore. Of course, there is no problem with paying these writers to have their work on line because they are all dead.

The site also features three additional pages that focus on

The greatest available novels of the 20th century
The greatest available Nobel Prize Winners
Available Pulitzer Prize Winning Books.

Here is a link to another interesting site
http://www.iblist.com/book23685.htm
On this site you can read even more stories: over 2,000 American short stories from writers as diverse as Shirley Jackson, Nathaniel Hawthorne, Jack London, Stephen Crane and, of course, again, the master of the horror story, Edgar Allan Poe.

Here are only a few of the stories you can read on this site:

"The Storm" by Kate Chopin
"The Yellow Wallpaper" by Charlotte Perkins Gilman
"The Middle Years" by Henry James
"In a Far Country" by Jack London
"The Little Regiment" by Stephen Crane
"A Journey" by Edith Wharton
"A Death in the Desert" by Willa Cather
"A Clean, Well-Lighted Place" by Ernest Hemingway
"An Alcoholic Case" by F. Scott Fitzgerald

These sites give you access to a multitude of books and short stories; far more than most of us could afford to buy so use them to 'dip' into books and short stories so that you're able to read as many diverse writers as possible. Writers should also be prolific readers so that the diversity of reading material will help us to develop our own style of writing.

Here are more interesting stories you might like to read.

'Classic'

Thomas Hardy	The Withered Arm
Honoré de Balzac	An Incident in the Reign of Terror
Ivan Turgenev	Torrents of Spring
Anton Chekhov	House with Mezzanine
Edgar Allan Poe	Pit & the Pendulum
Henry James	The Figure in the Carpet
James Joyce	The Dead
Joseph Conrad	The Secret Sharer
Leo Tolstoy	The Death of Ivan Ilyich
Nikolai Gogol	Diary of a Madman
D H Lawrence	The Prussian Officer
Franz Kafka	In the Penal Colony

Women Writers	
Kate Chopin	Desiree's Baby
Elizabeth Taylor	The Devastating Boys
Muriel Spark	Bang Bang You're Dead
Jean Rhys	Let Them Call It Jazz
Flannery O'Connor	A Good Man Is Hard To Find
Katherine Mansfield	Prelude
Helen Dunmore	Ice Cream
Grace Paley	Later the Same Day
Susan Hill	The Boy Who Taught The Bee-keeper To Read
Doris Lessing	The Habit Of Loving
Helen Simpson	Heavy Weather
Cynthia Ozick	The Suitcase
Ali Smith	Paradise
Jackie Kay	The Mirrored Twins
Beryl Bainbridge	Clap Hands, Here Comes Charlie

Rumer Godden	To Uncle with Love
Clare Boylan	Not a Recommended Hobby
	For A Housewife
A.S. Byatt	The July Ghost

Male Writers

Ernest Hemingway	Hills Like White Elephants
R K Narayan	Naga
James Baldwin	Sonny's Blues
Raymond Carver	Cathedral
John McGahern	Peaches
T.C. Boyle	Greasy Lake
John Updike	The Afterlife
Richard Ford	Abyss
China Mieville	Reports of Certain Events in London
Donald Barthelme	The Indian Uprising
Tim Winton	The Turning
Frank O'Connor	The Genius

At first, you will be intimidated after reading published short stories. I've heard students say many times – 'I'll never write like that.' Of course, you won't. You're unique, so find your unique voice from your own memories, your research, dreams and ideas. Use your past and present experiences to inform your future stories; use other people's past and present experiences and then exaggerate both subtly.

Remember: once you have learned how to make your reader wait with anticipation for your small nuggets of intriguing complications, you'll be writing great short stories.

Email to tell me when they're published at writingunderwater@tiscali.co.uk. I look forward to reading them.

Last Words

'Cherish your visions; cherish your ideals; cherish the music that stirs in your heart, the beauty that forms in your mind, the loveliness that drapes your purest thoughts, for out of them will grow delightful conditions, all heavenly environment; of these if you but remain true to them, your world will at last be built.'

James Allen – "As A Man Thinketh"

'On Broadway it was still bright afternoon and the gassy air was almost motionless under the leaden spokes of sunlight, and sawdust footprints lay about the doorways of butcher shops and fruit stores. And the great, great crowd, the inexhaustible current of millions of every race and kind pouring out, pressing round, of every age, of every genius, possessors of every human secret, antique and future, in every face the refinement of one particular motive or essence.'

Saul Bellow - "Seize the Day"

'To see a hillside white with dogwood bloom is to know a particular ecstasy of beauty, but to walk the gray Winter woods and find the buds which will resurrect that beauty in another May is to partake of continuity.'

Hal Borland, "New York Times", November 28, 1948

'The true beloveds of this world are in their lover's eyes, lilacs opening, ship lights, school bells, a landscape, remembered conversations, friends, a child's Sunday, lost voices, one's favorite suit, autumn and all seasons, memory, yes, it being the earth and water of existence, memory.'

Truman Capote - "Other Voices, Other Rooms"

'A tearing wind last night. A flurry of red clouds, hard, a water colour mass of purple and black, soft as a water ice, then hard slices of intense green stone, blue stone and a ripple of crimson light.'

Virginia Woolf, in her diary, August 17, 1938

'A word is not a crystal, transparent and unchanged; it is the skin of a living thought, and may vary greatly in color and content according to the circumstances and the time in which it is used.'

Oliver Wendell Holmes, "Towne v. Eisner", January 7, 1918

'Somewhere there was once a Flower, a Stone, a Crystal, a Queen, a King, a Palace, a Lover and his Beloved, and this was long ago, on an Island somewhere in the ocean 5,000 years ago ... Such is Love, the Mystic Flower of the Soul. This is the Center, the Self.'

Carl Jung

'The mind I love must have wild places, a tangled orchard where dark damsons drop in the heavy grass, an overgrown little wood, the chance of a snake or two, a pool that nobody's fathomed the depth of, and paths threaded with flowers planted by the mind.'

Katherine Mansfield

'We grow great by dreams. All big men are dreamers. They see things in the soft haze of a spring day or in the red fire of a long winter's evening. Some of us let these great dreams die, but others nourish and protect them; nurse them through bad days till they bring them to the sunshine and light which comes always to those who sincerely hope that their dreams will come true.'

Woodrow Wilson

BOOKS

O is a symbol of the world, of oneness and unity. In different cultures it also means the "eye," symbolizing knowledge and insight. We aim to publish books that are accessible, constructive and that challenge accepted opinion, both that of academia and the "moral majority."

Our books are available in all good English language bookstores worldwide. If you don't see the book on the shelves ask the bookstore to order it for you, quoting the ISBN number and title. Alternatively you can order online (all major online retail sites carry our titles) or contact the distributor in the relevant country, listed on the copyright page.

See our website **www.o-books.net** for a full list of over 500 titles, growing by 100 a year.

And tune in to myspiritradio.com for our book review radio show, hosted by June-Elleni Laine, where you can listen to the authors discussing their books.

mySpiritRadio